AF413641

272 Fun Activities for Toddlers

A Fun Toddler Activity Guide for Developing Motor Skills, Learning Critical Thinking, and Improving Emotional Regulation

Table of Contents

Part 1: The Activity Guide for Toddlers

171 Low Prep Toddler Activities for Sparking Creativity, Developing Motor Skills, and Having Fun Together

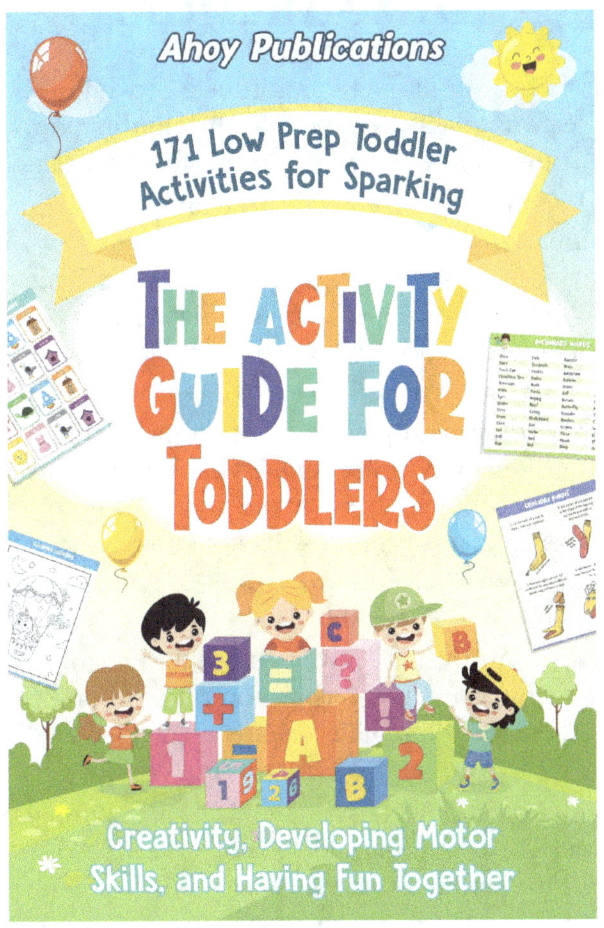

Introduction

Did you know that 90% of brain growth happens before age 5, while the rest of the brain continues to develop until the mid-20s? Creativity plays a major role during this period of rapid growth. It nurtures the development of nerve cell connections, which are crucial for motor and fine skills.

In this book, you will find sensory play activities and understand how they contribute to a child's cognitive, physical, and emotional growth. You'll also understand how music and dance can finetune their motor skills and find activities to instill a love for art and creativity in your child. A child's creativity and blooming motor skills allow them to walk, jump, dance, run, and coordinate their hand-eye movement. Their fine motor skills are responsible for their ability to write, draw, and handle small tools. Creativity is what propels a child to put these skills to use, allowing them to develop further.

A child who is curious to paint, draw, and play using different materials and tools will experience finer and more rapid development in their fine motor skills. Children should practice using pencils, tearing, molding, and cutting in a safe environment from a young age. These activities will prepare them for fundamental life skills, such as writing, using spoons, forks, knives, and tying shoelaces. In the following chapters, you'll find a range of ideas, from energetic outdoor games to calm indoor activities, that will allow your toddler to explore their physical capabilities in a fun and safe way.

Reading to your child, playing improv games with them, and acting and creating characters together can teach them much about verbal and non-verbal communication. Chapter 5 suggests activities to unleash your toddler's imagination and ultimately inspire their love for theater, literature, and reading. These games will also improve their comprehension skills and confidence.

The activities found in this book will teach your child that nature is the best place to turn to for therapy, creativity, and inspiration. You'll find ideas you can try with your child to stimulate their observational skills and physical development in the great outdoors. They'll learn to interact with nature meaningfully, enriching their sensory experiences and boosting their mental and emotional health.

If your toddler has always been curious about the kitchen, this is your opportunity to channel their interest into experimentation and hands-on learning experiences. From involving them in cooking to creating simple chemical reactions, chapter 7 is all about having fun in the kitchen. Finally, you'll find strategies you can use to help your child develop their social skills and make the most out of their quiet time.

Chapter 1: Sensory Play and Its Benefits

Toddlers use their basic senses of smell, touch, sound, and vision to explore the world around them. Sensory play involves letting your toddler indulge in activities that stimulate their minds and assist in developing their cognitive, emotional, and social skills. These activities include using soft materials like playdough, making different sensory bags to engage their senses, water play, and much more. Sensory play lets your toddler feel different textures, sensations, and materials, allowing them to map relevant information in their brain and better navigate the world around them.

Sensory play can improve your toddler's skills.

These activities can drastically improve fine motor skills, boost problem-solving abilities, increase hand-eye coordination, and heighten their senses. By providing a safe and stimulating environment for sensory play, parents and caregivers can support toddlers' overall growth and provide them with valuable opportunities for exploration and learning.

The Importance of Engaging Your Child's Senses through Play

Introducing your toddler to sensory play can do wonders for their development. From language development to emotional growth, sensory play can directly contribute to various cognitive skills.

Language Development

Through sensory play, your toddler can increase their pace of language development. When they engage in sensory play activities, toddlers will most likely describe their feelings in their own words. They will try to associate relevant words with their sensory experiences. Parents can also engage in conversations during playtime, providing them with appropriate vocabulary and asking them open-ended questions so they can express their feelings. These activities allow your toddler to expand their vocabulary, improve communication skills, and learn to associate words with objects.

Sensory Integration

This is *the ability to process sensory information and make sense of it*. Toddlers will receive sensory inputs, which the brain will naturally process. Your toddler's senses of touch, smell, taste, and sight provide sensory data to the brain. Through sensory play, they learn to understand and interpret this information, developing a better understanding of their environment. This integration enhances their ability to focus, concentrate, and engage in tasks that require multiple sensory inputs.

Creativity and Imagination

Your child's creativity and imagination will be boosted through sensory play. At this age, letting their imagination run wild and encouraging creativity will lay the foundation for better cognitive development and increase their problem-solving skills. Parents can provide children with materials like playdough (to make different shapes) and sensory bins (shallow bins filled with rice, beans, sand, and other objects) and encourage them to use their imagination. You can create play scenarios and role-playing games that will foster their problem-solving skills, divergent thinking capability, and improved cognitive flexibility.

Sensory Regulation

Over time, sensory play aids your toddler in regulating their sensory experiences and responding accordingly. Most toddlers are hypersensitive to loud noises, whereas some children might not have problems with loud noise and require a higher sensory input to react the same way. Repeated sensory play and exposing your toddler to varying stimuli allows them to explore and understand the threshold of their senses. Understanding the limitations of their reasons enables your toddler to better manage their sensory sensitivities through self-calming activities.

Multisensory Learning

As toddlers age, their ability to create neural connections improves daily. Nurturing an environment that promotes meaningful sensory play from a young age can work wonders. With multiple senses engaged, they will develop solid neural connections, enhancing memory retention and the ability to process information better.

Cognitive Growth

Engaging your toddler in these sensory play activities is crucial for brain growth and cognitive development. Having them feel different textures, visualize colors, smell, and hear sounds allows their brains to better understand the world around them. These sensory inputs also improve problem-solving skills and enhance cognitive flexibility and critical thinking abilities. For example, when you provide your toddler with sensory bins filled with various materials, they will naturally learn to recognize how they feel and smell; then, they can categorize them in their mind. The brain connects several sensory inputs linked with the object, creating spatial awareness. Sensory play also encourages curiosity, exploration, and discovery, which foster a love for learning.

Physical Growth

Sensory play activities involve hands-on exploration, encouraging children to use fine and gross motor skills. As toddlers manipulate objects, pour, scoop, squeeze, and mold materials, they develop hand-eye coordination, fine motor control, and muscle strength. When a child engages in finger painting, they refine their fine motor skills as they grasp and manipulate the paintbrush, improving their hand and finger dexterity. Likewise, water play activities like pouring water into different containers promote hand-eye coordination and increase spatial awareness. Activities like jumping into a ball pit or crawling through a sensory tunnel promote gross motor skills and overall physical development.

Emotional Growth

Sensory play significantly impacts a child's emotional well-being. Engaging in sensory experiences allows children to regulate their emotions and provides a safe outlet for self-expression. It can be calming and soothing, reducing anxiety and stress. For example, playing with kinetic sand or squeezing stress balls can release tension and aid in managing your child's emotions. Sensory play also allows children to explore their senses and discover what they enjoy, empowering them to make choices and express preferences. This sense of control and autonomy boosts self-confidence, self-esteem, and emotional resilience.

The following are different sensory play exercises you can do with your child.

1. Sensory Bin Exploration

A sensory bin can be any soft container filled with various materials like rice, beans, sand, or water-based jelly beads. Children can interact with these materials using their hands, scoops, and small play tools. They will most likely run their fingers through, feeling the different textures, and experiment with handling these materials using pouring and scooping tools.

This stimulates their sense of touch and promotes fine motor skills as they manipulate objects.

Materials:

- Large plastic container
- Various materials (rice, beans, sand, water beads, etc.),
- Scoops
- Small containers
- Small toys

Instructions:

1. Fill the container with different sensory materials (beans, rice, etc.).
2. Place the container on a mat or towel for easy cleaning later on.
3. Let your child explore the textures, pour, scoop, and manipulate the materials using the provided tools and toys.
4. Encourage them to use their hands and fingers to feel the textures and engage in imaginative play.

2. Playdough Creations

Playdough can enhance fine motor skills.
https://www.pexels.com/photo/children-playing-with-clay-8422174/

Playdough provides a distinct sensory experience as the material can be shaped, molded, and crafted into different shapes and objects using their hands and assistive tools like cookie cutters and rolling pins. Their sense of touch activates as they squeeze, squish, and flatten the playdough. This enhances their fine motor skills, hand-eye coordination, and creativity as they transform the playdough into various objects or characters.

Materials:

- Homemade or store-bought playdough
- Cookie cutters
- Rolling pins

Instructions:

1. Provide playdough and tools to your child to create new shapes and use tools to mold objects or characters using their imagination and fine motor skills.
2. Encourage them to use their hands to mold the play dough into different shapes.
3. They can use cookie cutters to make shapes or create their own designs.
4. Let them explore the different tools and experiment with different sizes and patterns.

3. Water Play

This activity is a refreshing and exploratory experience where children can pour, splash, and play with water using different water-holding objects like funnels, sponges, and cups. They can observe the water flow, watch how the water changes as they pour it from the main container, and develop an understanding of cause and effect. You will trigger their senses of touch, sight, and sound through water play while promoting gross motor skills and hand-eye coordination.

Materials:

- Basin
- Bathtub
- Water
- Cups
- Funnels
- Sponges
- Floating toys

Instructions:

1. Set up a safe water play area using a basin or bathtub.
2. Fill it with an appropriate amount of water.
3. Provide cups, funnels, sponges, and floating toys.
4. Let your child experiment by splashing, pouring, and transferring water between containers.
5. Encourage them to use the tools to experiment with the flow of water. Make sure to supervise them at all times.

4. Sensory Bags

These soft bags are pre-filled with different materials, allowing your child to experience tactile stimulation. When your child engages with the bag, they will most likely squeeze it, manipulate it into different shapes, and map different textures and shapes in their brain. Sensory bags are particularly useful for babies and toddlers who may still put objects in their mouths as they can experience the textures and sensations safely.

Safety Guide:

Always supervise your baby or toddlers when using sensory bags, as the seal may accidentally open, allowing the objects inside to be swallowed!

Materials:

- Resealable plastic bags
- Various items for sensory stimulation (colored gel, pom-poms, buttons, small toys, etc.).

Instructions:

1. Fill the bags with different sensory items, ensuring they are tightly sealed. You can use colored gel, pom-poms, buttons, or small toys.
2. Let your child press, squeeze, and manipulate the objects inside the bag, observing textures, colors, and shapes.

5. Nature Scavenger Hunt

Going on a nature hunt allows children to engage with their surroundings and explore the sensory aspects of the natural world. They can collect items like leaves, feathers, stones, or flowers, feel the different textures, observe the colors, and smell the scents. This activity connects children with nature and encourages curiosity and observation skills.

Materials:

- Basket or container
- Nature identification guide

Instructions:

1. Take your child on a nature walk in a safe outdoor environment such as a park or garden.
2. Provide them with a basket or container to collect items from nature, such as leaves, feathers, stones, or flowers.
3. Encourage them to touch and feel the different textures, observe the colors and shapes, and smell the scents of the collected items.
4. You can use a nature identification guide to teach them about different plants and objects they discover.

6. Sensory Painting

Sensory painting stimulates the senses of touch and sight.
https://www.pexels.com/photo/person-tracing-his-hand-on-paper-8612988/

Sensory painting involves using different materials and techniques to create textured artwork. Children can use brushes, sponges, or even their fingers to apply paint, exploring different strokes and textures. They can mix colors, create patterns, and experiment with different effects. Sensory painting stimulates their sense of touch, sight, and creativity.

Materials:

- Large paper
- Non-toxic paint
- Brushes,
- Sponges

Instructions:

1. Set up a designated painting area and place a large piece of paper on the floor or table.
2. Provide non-toxic paint in various colors and brushes.
3. You can also provide sponges or encourage your child to use their fingers.
4. Let them explore different painting techniques by making brush strokes, stamping with sponges, or finger-painting.
5. Encourage them to mix colors, experiment with textures, and create unique artwork.

7. Sensory Sound Jars

Sensory sound jars are filled with small objects that produce different sounds when shaken. Children can listen to the jars and identify the sounds they hear, enhancing their auditory perception and discrimination skills. They can also experiment with combining different objects to create unique sounds.

Materials:

- Empty plastic bottles
- Various small objects (rice, dried beans, buttons, bells, etc.)

Instructions:

1. Collect empty plastic bottles of different sizes and fill them with small objects. You can fill one with rice, another with dried beans, and another with buttons or bells.
2. Make sure that the bottles are sealed tightly.
3. Encourage your child to shake the bottles and listen to the sounds produced. Discuss the differences in sounds, such as the gentle rustling of rice versus the clattering of buttons.
4. They can experiment with combining different bottles to create different auditory effects.

8. Sensory Storytime:

Sensory storybooks engage multiple senses by incorporating touch and the other senses. Children can feel different textures within the book, lift flaps, or press buttons to activate sounds. This interactive experience enhances their engagement with the story and promotes sensory exploration.

Materials:

- Storybooks with textured pages or interactive features

Instructions:

1. Choose storybooks with textured pages or interactive features that engage multiple senses.
2. Sit with your child and read the books together.
3. Encourage them to touch and feel the different textures within the book, lift flaps, or press buttons to activate sounds or other interactive elements.
4. As you read, discuss the textures and sensations they experience, and ask questions to engage them in the story.

9. Bubble Play:

Bubbles provide a visual delight and tactile sensation for children. They can blow bubbles using wands or even their hands and pop them, experiencing the texture and feel on their skin. This activity stimulates their sense of sight, touch, and hand-eye coordination.

Materials:

- Bubble solution
- Bubble wands
- Straws
- Bubble machines

Instructions:

1. Prepare a bubble solution in a shallow container or use a bubble machine.
2. Provide wands or straws for blowing bubbles.
3. Show them how to dip the wand in the solution, blow gently, and create bubbles.
4. Encourage them to chase and pop the bubbles, feeling the gentle touch of the bubbles on their skin.
5. You can also create larger bubbles by using a straw to blow through a loop of string.

10. Sensory Obstacle Course:

A sensory obstacle course incorporates various sensory elements into physical activities. Children can crawl through tunnels, balance on beams, and navigate textured surfaces. This activity promotes gross motor skills, coordination, and body awareness while engaging multiple senses.

Materials:

- Pillows
- Cushions
- Tunnels
- Balance beams
- Textured mats

Instructions:

1. Set up an obstacle course using pillows, cushions, tunnels, balance beams, and textured mats.
2. Create a path that incorporates different sensory elements. For example, place pillows on the floor for your child to crawl or jump over, set up a tunnel to crawl through, or lay down a balance beam with textured mats.
3. Encourage your child to navigate the course, engaging their senses of touch, balance, and body awareness.
4. They can explore different textures, surfaces, and movements while developing their gross motor skills and coordination.

11. Sensory Scavenger Hunt:

A sensory scavenger hunt involves finding items based on their sensory qualities, such as smooth, rough, soft, or cold. Children can search for items within their environment and collect them in a container. This activity encourages observation skills, categorization, and exploration of different sensory attributes.

Materials:

- Container for collected items

Instructions:

1. Create a list of sensory items for your child to find within your home or garden. The list can include items with specific textures or sensory qualities, such as smooth, rough, soft, or cold to the touch.
2. Give your child a container to collect the items they find. Encourage them to touch and feel each item, describing its sensory qualities.
3. Help them categorize the collected items based on their sensory attributes.

12. Sand Play:

Sand can provide a rich sensory experience.
https://www.pexels.com/photo/little-boy-playing-in-the-sand-6459/

Playing with sand provides a tactile and rich sensory experience. Children can dig, pour, and mold sand, feeling the texture and exploring its properties. They can build sandcastles, create patterns, or even bury objects to discover and uncover. Sand play stimulates their sense of touch, promotes fine motor skills, and encourages imaginative play.

Materials:

- A sandbox or tray
- Sand
- Buckets
- Shovels
- Molds

Instructions:

1. Set up a sandbox or use a large tray filled with clean sand.
2. Provide buckets, shovels, and molds for your child to dig, pour, and shape it.

3. Encourage them to use their hands to feel the texture of the sand, build sandcastles, or create patterns.

4. They can experiment with pouring and transferring sand between containers.

5. Let their imagination guide their play as they explore all the different things they can do with the sand.

13. Sensory I-Spy Bottles:

Sensory I-Spy bottles are clear bottles filled with rice or other small objects. Children can shake the bottles and locate hidden items based on sight and sound. This activity enhances visual perception, auditory distinctions, and focus.

Materials:

- Clear plastic bottles
- Rice
- Small objects
- Trinkets

Instructions:

1. Take clear plastic bottles and fill them with rice or other small objects like buttons, beads, or trinkets.
2. Make sure that the bottles are tightly sealed.
3. Show your child the bottles and discuss what objects might be hidden inside.
4. Let them shake the bottles and listen to the sounds produced.
5. Encourage them to find and identify the hidden objects by carefully turning and tilting the bottles.
6. They can engage their sense of sight and sound as they search for and locate the items.

14. Sensory Kitchen Play:

Sensory kitchen play involves providing safe food items like rice, flour, or pasta for children to explore and manipulate. They can pour, stir, and measure ingredients using different kitchen tools. This activity promotes sensory exploration, fine motor skills, and imaginative play as they pretend to cook or bake.

Materials:

- Mixing bowls
- Utensils
- Measuring cups
- Safe food items like rice, flour, and pasta

Instructions:

1. Set up a safe play area in the kitchen using mixing bowls, utensils, and safe food items like rice, flour, or pasta.
2. Let your child explore and manipulate the ingredients using their hands or kitchen utensils.
3. They can pour, stir, and measure the items, experiencing different textures and sensory qualities.
4. Encourage imaginative play by pretending to cook or bake.

5. Supervise closely to make sure they don't ingest any raw ingredients.

15. Sensory Music Exploration:

Children can engage in sensory-rich music activities by combining musical instruments with textured objects like fabric or feathers and moving to the rhythm of the music. This activity stimulates auditory perception, coordination, and kinesthetic learning while providing tactile and auditory sensory experiences.

Materials:

- Musical instruments
- Various textured objects like fabric, feathers, and bells

Instructions:

1. Provide a variety of musical instruments such as drums, shakers, or bells. Put out textured objects like fabric, feathers, or bells.
2. Play recorded music or sing songs together.
3. Encourage your child to explore musical instruments and experiment with creating sounds and rhythms.
4. They can also incorporate textured objects into their music-making by shaking or rubbing them.
5. Let them move to the rhythm of the music, feeling the vibrations and engaging their senses of sound and touch.

Chapter 2: Arts, Crafts, and Creativity

Do you remember how much you loved painting and creating things as a child? Arts and crafts are fun activities that all children enjoy. Children gravitate toward Lego, playdough, and crayons from a very young age. They don't even understand what they are, but something inside seems to drive them toward these toys! That's their creativity. This raises the question: *Are all children born creative?*

Children tend to like arts and crafts activities.

In 1968, NASA researched the creativity level of their engineers and scientists. Dr. Beth Jarman and Dr. George Land led this research, and the results filled them with curiosity. They wanted to find out if all people are born creative, so they used the same tests on children. They were surprised by what they discovered. A large percentage of the children scored high in the imagination category. They repeated the tests on the same children when they turned ten and found only 30% of them scored high, and another time when they were fifteen, to find that only 12% of them managed to do it again.

Dr. Jarman and Dr. Land concluded that children are creative by nature. Their creativity ends up being suppressed by either their parents or at school.

The parent's job is cultivating and nourishing this gift in their children. This chapter covers the role of arts and crafts in developing your child's self-expression, motor skills, and creativity. You will also find entertaining and artistic activities that instill a love of arts and crafts in your child.

The Role of Arts and Crafts in Your Child's Development

Your child isn't too young to learn anything. In fact, you should instill certain traits in them from a very young age. Arts and crafts play a considerable role in their development and can affect every aspect of their life.

Enhance Creativity

Children have a vast imagination, and art is the perfect outlet to express this gift and enhance their creativity. Many children develop their creativity through art, allowing them to try new things, think outside the box, and express themselves.

However, don't expect your child's drawing to be good. Parents need to differentiate between talent and creativity. Creativity isn't about doing a good job; it's about discovering, exploring, imagining, and thinking. Focus on the process and not the end result.

Improve Motor Skills

Arts and crafts involve using hands, which improves your child's motor skills and facilitates the movement of their muscles. These activities are easy and fun and give your child the freedom to do whatever they want, allowing their motor skills to develop faster. Some artistic exercises like origami, painting, and drawing can improve your child's muscle memory and hand-to-eye coordination. Once your child improves their motor skills, they can gain independence and start to eat, shower, go to the bathroom, and tie their shoelaces on their own.

Encourage Self-Expression

Children observe and take in everything that goes on around them. Some can be vocal and find it easy to express themselves about the world they are still exploring, while others can be shy and struggle with self-expression. These children need to communicate their feelings and ideas through visual outlets like arts and crafts. These activities provide them with a safe space where they feel in control and can create whatever they want using the tools of their choice.

They can also express their innermost feelings and thoughts going on in their subconscious. If you want a better idea of what goes on in your child's mind, look at what they paint or create.

Now that you know the benefits of arts and crafts in your child's development, it's time to introduce them to fun exercises to boost their creativity.

16. Making a Collage

Materials:

- Scissors
- Glue
- Paper
- Pictures of their choice

- Fabric or ribbons

- Glitter, foil, or tinsel

- Sand, feathers, leaves, or any object from nature

- Buttons, paperclips, or ice cream sticks

Safety Guide:

Be careful when your child uses scissors. Sit next to them and provide instructions. If they can't use it, either hold their hand while they are cutting (or cut for them.)

A collage will help a child express themselves.
https://pxhere.com/en/photo/773788

Instructions:

1. Place all the tools on a tray and sit with your child at a table.
2. Let them create the collage themselves and choose the tools they want to use. For instance, they might want to use paper and leaves to create a garden or a forest or use colorful paper to create a pattern.
3. Encourage and praise them at every step.
4. After they choose the pictures, either one of you can cut and stick them on the paper using glue.
5. Then, they can decorate the collage with any of the materials.

17. Playdough Creativity

Materials:

- Playdough
- Rolling pins, plastic knives, or cookie cutters
- Toys like baking equipment, cars, or plastic animals

Instructions:

1. Allow your child to experiment with the playdough a little.
2. Show them how to flatten, stretch, and roll it.
3. Hand your child different toys and encourage them to use them to create patterns or shapes.
4. You can try roleplaying games. Your child can be the baker, and you are the customer. They can make cookies with the playdough and serve them to you.
5. They can also use it to make different shapes. Let their imagination run wild.

18. Handprint/Footprint Art

Materials:

- White cardstock
- Blue cardstock
- Different colors of acrylic paint
- Paint brushes
- Scissors
- Glue
- Googly eyes
- Black marker
- Green tissue paper
- Baby wipes

Instructions:

1. Encourage your child to use the paint and the paintbrush to color their hands or feet. If they are too young, you can do it for them.
2. Then, ask them to press their hands or feet over the white cardstock.
3. Give them a wet wipe to clean and let them do it again with different paint colors.
4. Using the scissors, help your child cut off every handprint from the white cardboard and stick them with the glue on the blue cardboard.
5. Cut the green tissue paper, let your child crinkle it up, and glue it on the blue cardboard.
6. They can also add googly eyes on the hands and even draw on them to make funny faces.

Safety Guide:

Watch your child closely to ensure they don't put the paint in their mouth.

19. Paper Crown

Materials:

- Colored craft paper
- Pencil
- Scissors
- Sticky tape
- Stickers

Instructions:

1. Encourage your child to draw a zigzag in the middle of the craft paper. If they can't, hold their hand and help them out.
2. Have them cut the paper down the line and give them a hand whenever they need help.
3. Ask them to attach the two ends of the paper with sticky tape.
4. They can then decorate it with stickers.
5. Finally, they can wrap it in a circle around their head to make sure it fits before attaching it with sticky tape.

PAPER CROWN

Glue here

Glue here

CUT & GLUE 1 CUT OUT  2 GLUE  USE EXAMPLE OR YOUR IMAGINATION 

20. Blot Art Hearts

Materials:

- Paintbrush
- Different paint colors
- Sturdy paper
- Scissors

Instructions:

1. Since this can be tricky for your child, cut the paper into the shape of a heart. You will need about ten hearts.
2. Encourage your child to add drops of different paint colors to one side of the heart using the paintbrush.
3. They should then fold the other half of the heart over the painted side and press on it hard.
4. Then, they will unfold the card and see their beautiful creation.
5. They can repeat the previous steps with the rest of the hearts.

21. Bubble Wrap Painting

Materials:

- Paper
- Different paint colors
- Foam rollers
- Paint brushes
- Sticky tape
- Bubble wrap

Instructions:

1. Stick the bubble wrap on a table using sticky tape.
2. Using a foam roller, let your child paint over the bubble wrap with different colors.
3. There shouldn't be a lot of paint on the bubble wrap's raised surface. If there is, ask your child to roll a lighter layer.
4. Now, you or an older child should place the paper on the bubble wrap and gently press on it from the middle outwards.
5. Then, your child can remove the paper and discover the beautiful art they created.

22. Painting with Wheels

Materials:

- Paint
- Cardboard
- Drop cloths
- Car and truck toys

Instructions:

1. Your child can practice this exercise indoors or in your backyard.
2. Spread the drop cloth on the floor, then add the cardboard and the car toys.
3. Prepare the paint by putting it on paper plates, baking sheets, or pizza pans.
4. Your child should cover the cars and trucks' wheels by rolling them over the paint.
5. Now, your child can paint the cardboard by rolling the cars over them.

23. Watercolor Resist Painting

Materials:

- Liquid paint
- Watercolor paper
- Crayons
- Paintbrush

Instructions:

1. Your child can draw any shape they want using crayons on watercolor paper.
2. Next, your child will paint over the crayon drawing with the paintbrush and liquid paint.
3. Leave it to dry and hang it on your fridge to show off your little one's painting.

Suncatchers

Materials:

- Tape
- Scissors
- Contact paper
- Yarn

Instructions:

1. Your child will cut the yarn into different lengths.
2. Using sticky tape, hang the contact paper on the lower part of a window so your child can reach it.
3. Your child will then throw the yarn on the sticky paper.

Safety Guidance:

If you live on a high floor, hang the contact paper on a door instead of a window.

24. Butterfly Kite

Materials:

- Shape templates
- Markers
- Stickers
- Ribbons

- Cardstock

- Crayons

- Glue

- Long string

Instructions:

1. Draw a butterfly on the cardstock using a butterfly shape template, then cut it out.

2. Now, it's your child's turn. Instruct them to draw different simple shapes to decorate the butterfly with the black marker. Help them out if they can't draw.

3. They should then color the shapes.

4. Using glue, your child will stick the ribbon at the butterfly's end.

5. Then, they will tape the string on the top of the butterfly.

6. Your child can go out in the backyard and fly their new kite.

25. Salt Painting

Materials:

- Template of any shape

- Watercolor paper

- Water

- Food coloring

- Salt

- Glue

- Pencil

Instructions:

1. Using a pencil, help your child trace the templates over the watercolor paper.

2. Help your child add glue to outline each shape.

3. Your child should then add salt to the glue. Remove any excess salt.

4. Leave the salt and glue to dry.

5. Add a small amount of water to the food coloring to turn it into watercolor paint.

6. Place the watercolor in the pipette and give it to your child to drip slowly over the glue and salt shapes.

7. Leave it overnight to dry.

26. Paper Plate Craft

Materials:

- Googly eyes

- Patty cases

- Crayons

- Scissors

- Paper plate
- Glue

Instructions:

1. Cut the paper plate into the shape of a fish.
2. Encourage your child to decorate their fish with different colors. Let them get creative.
3. Cut the patty cases to make scales, and let your child stick them on the fish with the glue.
4. Finally, they should stick the googly eyes on the fish.

27. Paper Cup Whale

Materials:

- Marker
- Scissors
- Pipe cleaners
- Googly eyes
- Glue
- Paper
- Tape
- Paper cup

Instructions:

1. Your child will cut small parts of the paper to make the fins, then stick them to the cup's side.
2. Your child should take two small pipe cleaners, bend them a little, and tape them on the bottom of the cup to make the tail.
3. They then need to turn the cup upside down, stick the googly eyes using glue, and draw a smiley face with a marker.

28. Egg Carton Caterpillar

Materials:

- Paper
- Googly eyes
- Pipe cleaner
- Paint brushes
- Paint
- Scissors
- Egg carton

Instructions:

1. Remove the cover of the egg carton, then cut the wells along it so your child has two pieces of the same length to work with.
2. Use scissors to make two small holes in the wells at the bottom or top of the carton.

3. Now, hand the carton to your child and let them paint. They can use any color they want and do it with a paintbrush or their fingers.

4. Cut the pipe cleaner in halves and bend them slightly from one end.

5. Give the pipe cleaners to your child and instruct them to insert each one from the straight end into the holes.

6. Your child should then stick the googly eyes on the carton.

29. Fork Flower Painting

Materials:

- Plate
- Paper
- Paintbrush
- Two different color paints
- Green paint
- Forks

Instructions:

1. Pour some green paint into a small bowl or a paper plate.

2. Your child should use the paintbrush and green color to paint the bottom of the paper to create grass.

3. Your child should then paint four flowers' stems and leaves over the grass.

4. Pour the two other paint colors into two different bowls.

5. Your child should dip the top part of one fork over one of the colors, then place it over two of the drawn stems to create flowers.

6. Tell them to repeat the previous step with the second color, then place it on the other two stems.

Arts and crafts are fun; you can do all these activities with your child to encourage and bond with them.

Chapter 3: Music, Dance, Rhythm, and Creativity

In this chapter, you will learn how music, dance, rhythm, and creativity can benefit your child's confidence and overall development.

Toddlers enjoy music and dancing.

Tap into the Rhythms of Life: Growing Your Child's Confidence and Development

Children love music. It makes them clap, jump, or shake their heads. Even when a child can barely form a word, they can respond to the sound of music. Here are five benefits of music and dancing:

1. **Physical Balance**

There's no better way to strengthen the mind and body than through dancing. When they dance, children learn to maintain their balance and flexibility. It also boosts their confidence, fitness level, and overall health in general.

2. **Emotional Growth**

Dance is an excellent way to relieve your child's stress and boost their overall mood. Try playing cheerful songs that would get them on their feet and keep them moving, for example, "Happy" by Pharrell Williams or "I Like to Move It, Move It."

3. **Social Maturity**

When you want to make a child socially aware and interactive, introduce them to dance activities. This would even be more fun when friends, the entire family, or a group of children their age are involved. "Kids or people, in general, tend to produce mirror neurons when they mimic the actions performed by others," according to published research from the Arts in Psychotherapy Journal. Children also tend to create a sense of attachment and social bonding when engaging with others. Dancing makes your child adopt good social skills and learn to share positive emotions with others.

4. **Development in Motor Skills**

Motor skills allow the use of your large and small body muscles. For example, using your hands and legs is a great way to develop your motor skills. Dancing is a brilliant way to encourage children to move their hands, legs, and body. So, whether it be clapping their hands, bending their little fingers around a tambourine, or crawling on their knees, they exercise their muscles.

5. **Sensory and Creativity Development**

Music is the best way to grow your child's creativity and senses. When a child dances to a rhythm, they learn to coordinate and contain their steps and actions with the provided space around them. Music helps their minds wander off to an imaginary world, but with dancing, they focus their sights on the physical world. With dance, the side of your child's brain that controls their emotions, movements, balance, memory, and images is greatly enhanced. Music is also a powerful way for children to express how they feel in creative ways, and the more they get engrossed in it, the more their creativity grows.

15 Activities to Enhance Your Child's Motor Skills and Emotional Expression

Here are 15 fun activities you can carry out with your child to build their motor skills and boost their confidence level through rhythms, creativity, music, and dance:

30. Musical Chairs

This is a classic musical activity. Each arranged chair must face the opposite side of the other. This activity is usually played with fewer chairs than the number of players; for example, if the number of players is five, there would only be four arranged chairs. This activity builds your child's self-awareness and keeps them in a position to be ready to quickly spot an empty chair.

For a less competitive game, make the number of chairs equal to the number of players. It's still a lot more fun that way too.

31. Musical Statues

This is a perfect music activity for your toddler. During a musical statue, your child learns to control their body while being asked to "freeze!" in mid-air. You play this by playing a song on your mobile phone or a CD, preferably for everyone to dance to. Then you pause the music and yell, "Freeze!" Everyone, including your toddler, must freeze immediately in their current dancing positions just as you pause the song. This would be so much fun for children when they all freeze together without any of them being disqualified.

32. What Instruments Do You Hear?

This game aims to teach listening with precision as you name the instruments you hear. To make it fun, ensure your child knows a range of musical instruments and how they sound. If you don't have any musical instruments around the house, you can play videos of them on YouTube.

33. Creating Homemade Musical Instruments

When looking for a way to draw your child's attention, try telling them about making one great musical instrument. Your child would not only want to make those instruments with you, but they'll also look forward to playing them. This builds your child's motor skills, creativity, and a good social and emotional bond with you. There are a variety of homemade musical instruments you can learn and make with your child:

- A tin can drum
- Paper straw panpipes
- An elastic band guitar

Starting a family band with these tools would be a great way to build bonds with your child and those around you. Children love it when they can make so much noise with drums, tambourines, and panpipes, especially those they crafted themselves.

PLASTIC EASTER EGG MARACAS

NEEDED MATERIALS:

Plastic Easter eggs
Plastic spoons
White tape
Popcorn kernels
Markers

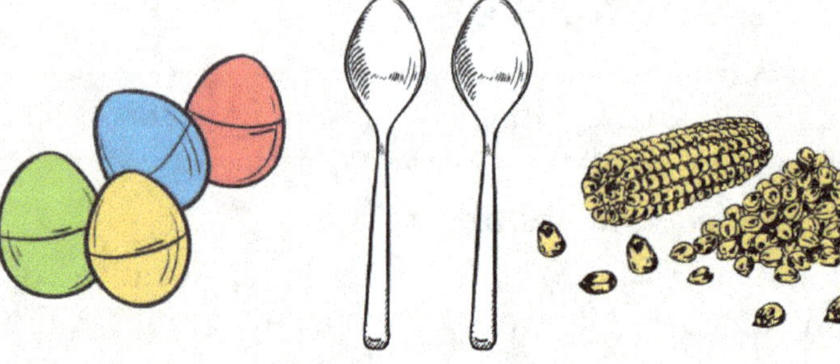

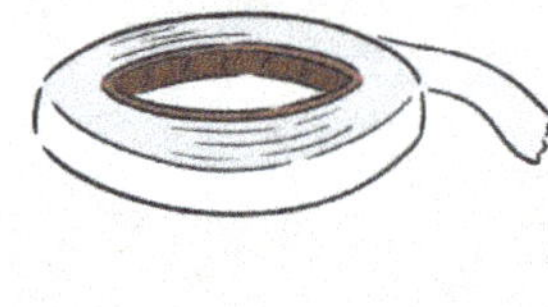

DIRECTIONS:

1. Fill the eggs with popcorn kernels.
2. Tape two plastic spoons on either side.
3. Tape the spoon ends together.
4. Decorate the tape with markers.

BALLOON SKIN DRUMS

NEEDED MATERIALS:

Small tin cans

Balloons

Scissors

Ribbon

Paint and brush

Craft or hot glue

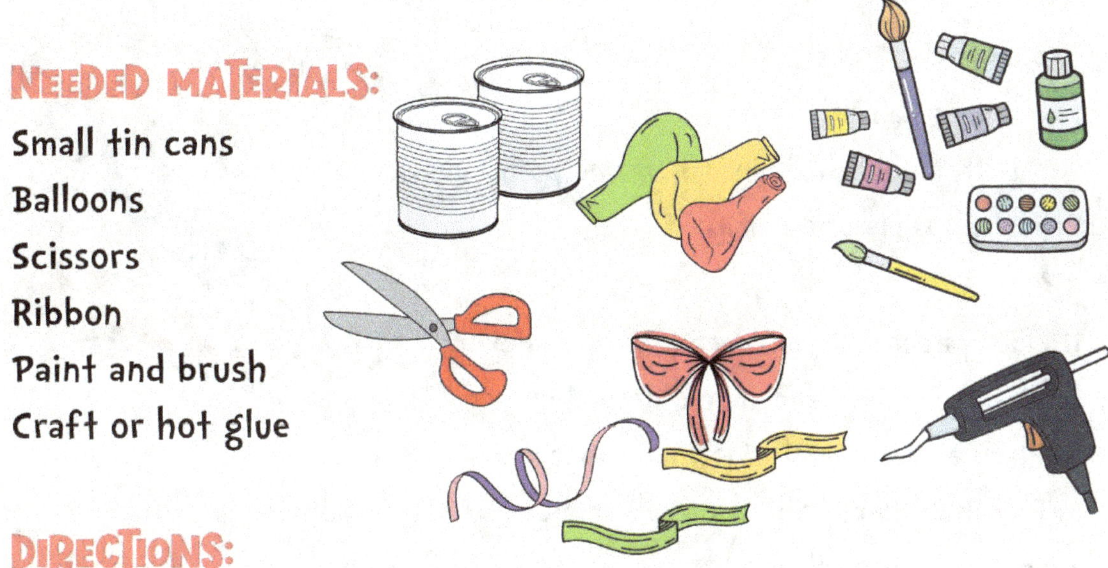

DIRECTIONS:

1. Wash, dry, and remove labels from the tin cans.

2. Paint can and/or decorate as desired.

3. Cut the balloon and stretch it over the tin can's opening.

4. Add ribbon to the seam of the balloon to help seal it in place and for decoration.

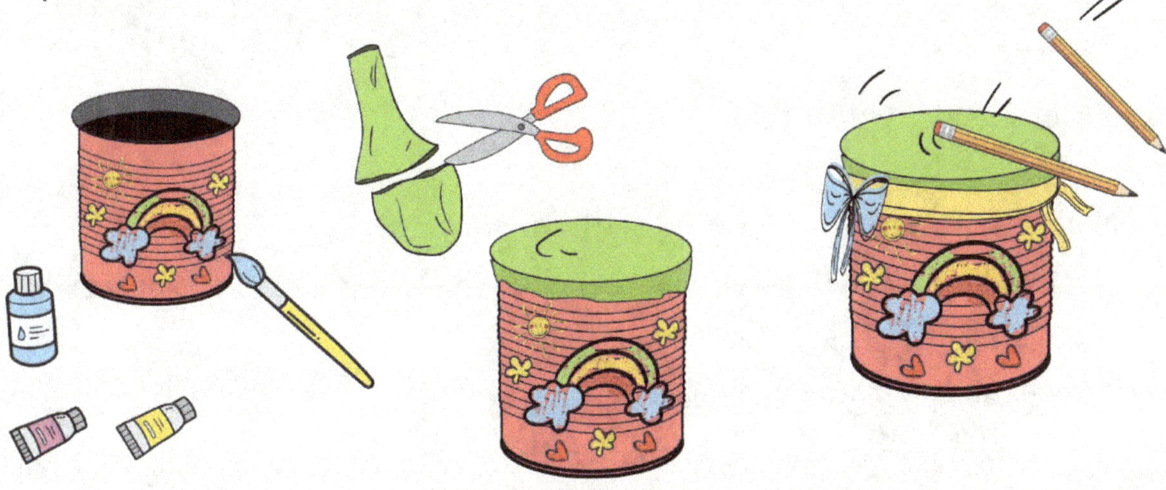

Popsicle Stick Harmonica

NEEDED MATERIALS:

two popsicle sticks

two rubber bands

two toothpicks cut the width of the popsicle stick

Paper (popsicle-sized strip)

DIRECTIONS:

1. Place paper strip between popsicle sticks.

2. Wrap a rubber band snugly around one end.

3. Place a toothpick inside the rubber band.

4. Put the other toothpick at the other end of the popsicle sticks and wrap it with the other rubber band.

Singing Straws

NEEDED MATERIALS:

six to eight straws

Sticky tape

Scissors

Colored paper (optional)

DIRECTIONS:

1. Cut the straws into different lengths in groups of two.

2. Cut a long piece of sticky tape and place the straws on the sticky side in twos, arranging them from shortest to longest.

3. Secure in place with additional tape.

4. Decorate with colored paper (optional).

34. Musical Packages

In this game of patience, items are wrapped with many layers of a newspaper sheet. They are then passed around to each participant of the game. Each person must unwrap a layer of the cover and pass it to the other person. It goes around like that in a circle until the last layer is unwrapped. Add a musical instrument like an egg shaker inside the wrap to make this more fun. This would build momentum and curiosity. Whichever child unwraps the final later gets to keep what's inside.

35. Party Freeze Song

Play a song and encourage your child to dance. The catch here is that they have to stop whenever you say so. Remember that these games depend on your child's age, which would determine their response. You should make a few demonstrations before they get the hint of it. This type of game sharpens listening and develops impulse skills. Say "stop" and then "dance" from time to time, and have them enjoy the fun of it.

36. Matching Sounds

You can start with pairs of homemade instruments. When you play an instrument, the goal is for your child to listen and search for something that can make the closest sound possible. Here are a few examples:

- A triangle produces a faint or sharp sound. Two spoons can make such a sound.
- Drums produce a deep sound. A box can make that sound, too.
- Cymbals produce a sharp sound. A pot lid can also do this.

There are no rules to playing this game. One person makes the suggested sound, and the other player goes looking.

37. Mimicking Steps

Here, all you need to do is to create a dance step while playing music and ask everyone, including your child, to repeat your moves. Do this game in turns and see how creative and fun it gets.

38. A Little Elephant

With this song, you can teach your child how to count and make sense of basic numbers. You can even take advantage of this opportunity and teach how to walk in a straight line. To play, place a string on the ground and begin by walking on it, using your arms for balance. Then, everyone can sing the lyrics together.

39. Draw Your Music

You'll need a large piece of paper and drawing pencils or crayons. Play a song and ask them to draw what they feel or hear. It could be a wavy line, a zigzag line, or a curved line. Make this an open-ended activity, and watch your children express themselves through what they hear. Make sure to draw yours as well.

40. Hide, Listen, and Spot

This game involves hearing sounds and guessing where they came from.

In this game, one of you is going to be blindfolded. The aim is to figure out where the sound is coming from. To play, blindfold your child and use whatever you have on hand, whether an instrument or household items, to produce sounds. Do that while moving away from them. When you get as far away as possible, hide and keep making sounds. Once you stop, that's their signal to come looking for you.

41. Sock Puppet Show

You can teach your child how to use a puppet to create a show. You can use various characters to play roles and express different emotions. The best part about this activity is that they can take as long as they want to create the puppets.

CROCODILE PUPPET

1. Cut the foot of a sock as shown. Turn sock inside out.

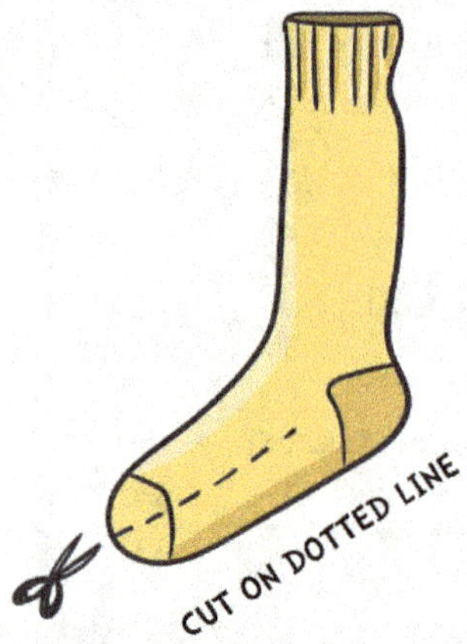

2. Cut a piece of red material in the shape of the opening and sew to sock with an overhand stitch.

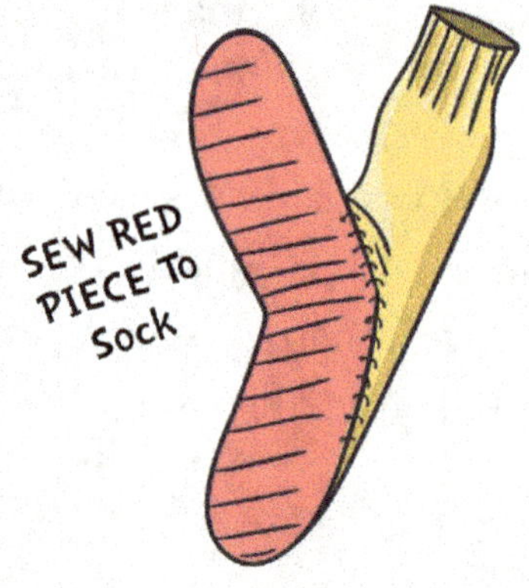

3. Turn sock right side out. Cut cardboard the same size as the red mouth. Fold and insert in sock.

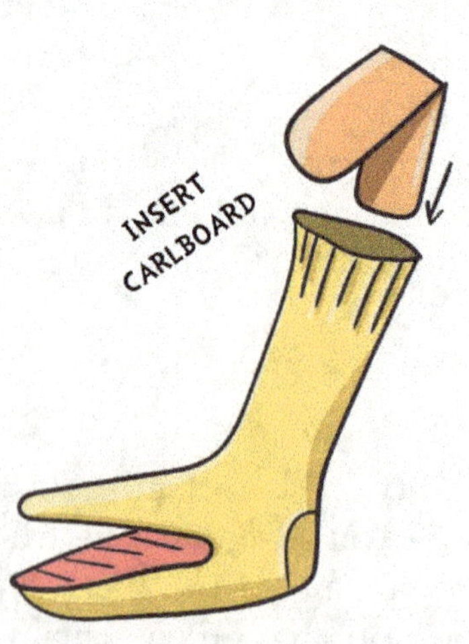

4. Add buttons for eyes and nose. Use yarn braids and curls for hair.

42. Dancing Scarves

Dancing with colorful scarves and ribbons opens up your child's imagination. It also builds their motor skill as they wave and move the scarfs around. To make this even more interesting for them, find rainbow scarves or ribbons and watch them swirl them around for what feels like ages. You can make a video and take pictures of them as they do this.

43. Marching to a Beat

Teach your child how to dance to the beats of a song by making certain gestures with their feet and hands. Show them how to lift their legs and arms high above the ground and back onto the floor, following the rhythm of the beats.

44. Head, Shoulders, Knees, and Toes

This activity is for children who can't keep still. Sing or talk "Head, Shoulders, Knees, and Toes" and move both your hands accordingly and have the child do the same.

The best way to bring out the creativity in your child is through music, dance, and rhythm. To improve your child's health and emotional growth, you can have them engage in activities like musical chairs, creating homemade instruments, matching sounds, and many more. Make the most of your time with your children, and make precious memories that will last you a lifetime.

Chapter 4: Let's Get Physical

This chapter is about fun activities that boost your toddler's physical development. You will never run out of options to keep your child happy and engaged.

As a parent, watching your little one grow and explore the world is one of the most rewarding parts of the job. Their energy seems boundless at this age, and you want to keep them active and engaged most of the time, which is the key to managing all that energy. The activities in this chapter are designed for toddlers - they're fun and creative and help build crucial skills like balance, coordination, and motor skills. Whether you're looking for an energetic outdoor game or a calm indoor activity for your child, this chapter has you covered.

Children tend to enjoy the outdoors.

Benefits of Outdoor Play vs. Indoor Play

Whether indoor play suits your taste better than outdoor play (or vice versa), the point to be made here is that the interest of the children comes first. Outdoor play offers a lot of benefits to children compared to indoor play.

Outdoor play makes room for more physical activities, which, in turn, allows children the opportunity to develop gross motor skills and improve their overall health. It also brings children closer to natural elements, like making contact with the sand to build sand castles or dig a ditch, thus helping them develop an appreciation for the environment. Interaction with nature also has a way of enhancing creativity, cognitive development, and problem-solving skills. This could be seen as a result of them trying to find new ways to build and decorate better sand castles.

Additionally, outdoor play encourages healthy self-esteem, social interaction, and teamwork, as outdoor recreation makes children engage in group activities and games to sometimes achieve a common goal. Being accepted among peers during such activities helps build a sense of belonging and appreciation for themselves.

Indoor play also has its advantages too. One such advantage includes creating a controlled environment for certain activities that don't necessarily need to be outdoors. Such activities include Lego-building, and this activity in itself fosters great imaginative play regardless of weather conditions.

Fun Outdoor Games for Children

At their age, toddlers are always eager to go outdoors. They are constantly curious about the world around them and want to explore it. So, getting them outside is always a great idea for more reasons beyond just *fun*. Getting outside with your toddler will also help them develop physically and mentally while having fun at the same time. These outdoor activities have a way of helping your child build up essential skills that they can quickly implement in school and other social situations. Also, it is no news that having your children play outside, in the warm sun and the cool breeze, has a lot of health benefits for them.

Here are some engaging outdoor games that have been put together to make your little one laugh, learn, and have fun.

45. **Obstacle Courses:** Set up a simple obstacle course in your backyard with hula hoops to jump in and out of, balls to crawl under, balloons to pop, and tunnels to crawl through. This builds balance, coordination, and motor skills.

46. **Bubble Blowing:** Bubbles are endlessly entertaining for toddlers and develop their hand-eye coordination and motor skills. Show your toddler how to gently blow into a bubble wand to make bubbles. Have them dip the wand in the solution, raise it to their mouth, and blow gently but steadily to produce a stream of bubbles. Make a challenge out of seeing who can blow the biggest bubble.

47. **Hopscotch:** Use chalk to draw a hopscotch board on the sidewalk. Have your toddler hop, jump, and balance as they go through the numbers. This helps with balance, motor skills, and counting.

48. **Catch and Release:** Gently toss a ball, beanbag, or other soft toy back and forth with your toddler. Start close together and slowly move further apart as their skills improve. This helps hand-eye coordination and motor skills.

49. **Follow the Leader:** Walk, run, hop, jump, spin, march, and have your toddler imitate your movements. Switch who plays leader now and then. This builds motor skills, balance, and coordination.

Being outside with your little one provides opportunities for learning and development while having fun. These simple activities will keep your toddler engaged and build crucial skills. Most of all, make sure to enjoy the special time together outside in nature.

Exciting Indoor Activities

Outdoor activities are great, but due to season changes, clashing schedules, and work, they're just not possible sometimes. The goal is to keep your toddler happy and always engaged—the where and how are unimportant as long as your child is excited and happy.

Indoor activities are a great way to stimulate your little one on rainy or chilly days. Having your toddler spend so much time inside might seem dreadful initially, but it can be an opportunity to bond. Toddlers have the energy to burn, so providing outlets to explore their physical skills indoors is vital for their development and your sanity! Here are some excellent indoor exercise options:

50. **Obstacle Courses:** If you can't set one up outside, you can do it inside. Set up a simple course with hula hoops, tunnels made from chairs, blankets, and pillows to crawl through, balls to roll and throw, and targets to aim for. You can even give your toddler the chance to be creative and have them design the course.

51. **Puzzles:** Have your toddler exercise their problem-solving, cognitive, and creative muscles with puzzles. This will sharpen their minds and allow them to have fun indoors. Completing the puzzle also instills a sense of accomplishment and pride, boosting their confidence levels for other tasks. You can get a store-bought puzzle or have them draw their own. That will put their creativity to the test. They can use a sturdy cardboard piece or a Bristol board.

52. **Stringing Items Together:** Stringing beads, pasta, cereal, or buttons together on yarn or string develops fine motor skills and hand-eye coordination in a fun, engaging way. Provide different-sized items for your toddler to manipulate and let them be creative in designing their necklaces or bracelets. Give them laces or strings and large wooden or plastic beads with holes big enough to fit through. Show them how to thread the lace through the bead hole and pull it through. Have them practice stringing the beads onto the lace. Start with larger beads, then progress to smaller ones as their skills improve. Display their creations proudly to motivate them to keep practicing.

53. **Play Music and Have a Dance Party:** Toddlers love moving to music. Put on some upbeat songs and dance together. Spin, jump, march, clap along - any energetic, full-body movements. Dancing also helps with balance, coordination, and body awareness.

54. **Hide and Seek:** This list will be incomplete without hide and seek to balance things. You and your child can take turns hiding and looking for one another around the house. To make it more fun, other family members can join in.

55. **Indoor Bowling:** Save time and the earth by using your old recyclable bottles to create a makeshift bowling set. Your indoor bowling rink is done by lining up 6 to 10 water bottles in your living room or at the end of the hall and taping the area to be used as the starting line. You can use cardboard boxes as bumpers as well. Grab an indoor ball, preferably medium-sized, and you are all set to bowl.

If the bottles don't stay fixed, adding some water will help you stabilize them. Just remember to screw the cap tightly to avoid any spills. You can purchase children's indoor bowling kits if you want something more practical.

56. **Simon Says:** The classic game of Simon Says is ideal for helping toddlers follow basic instructions and learn body awareness. Give simple commands like "Simon says jump up and down" or "Simon says touch your nose." Toddlers must follow the commands when you say, "Simon says," and not follow commands without that phrase. This game helps toddlers develop listening skills, understand the meanings of words for different body parts and movements, and control their bodies.

57. **Hot Potato:** This is another fun activity to get them all excited and giggling. You only need a softball or a bean bag, acting as the hot potato, to start things. While everyone sits in a circle, music is played in the background as you take turns passing the item as fast as possible to the person next to them. Anyone holding the potato when the music stops is eliminated. Keep at it until there is only one player left.

58. **Touch-and-Feel Box:** This game will have your child making all the strangest faces; you do not want to miss it! Also, it is a great way to improve their sensory skills. For this game, you will need a shoe box or any other box with a lid. Make a hole the size of your child's hand on one side of the box, place an item in it, and cover it with the lid. Have your child put their hand through the hole you made to guess what you set in the box. This will keep your child's mind sharp and active as they try to determine what you have placed in the box. You can also make it more fun by asking them questions about the item or dropping clues to help them.

With just some simple props and enough enthusiasm, these indoor activities will have your toddler giggling, moving, and mastering new skills in no time. They also provide opportunities for bonding and joyful interaction between you two.

Developing Motor Skills through Play

Playtime is a learning opportunity for toddlers. Their bodies and minds are developing rapidly, and playing builds the motor skills and coordination they'll use for the rest of their lives.

Outdoor Play

Riding a tricycle can strengthen your toddler's leg muscles.
https://www.pexels.com/photo/boy-riding-green-bike-1058501/

Playing outside gives toddlers the chance to strengthen their muscles and improve balance. This includes activities like:

59. Going to the Playground: Swings, slides, and climbing structures build leg and core strength.

60. Playing with Balls: Throwing, kicking, and chasing balls improve hand-eye coordination and balance.

61. Riding Tricycles: Pedaling strengthens leg muscles and improves motor skills. Look for tricycles with handrails for support.

62. Playing Make-Believe: Pretending to be animals walking on all fours, jumping like frogs, or flying like birds builds muscle control and flexibility.

Indoor Play

There are lots of fun indoor activities for developing motor skills:

63. Building Blocks: Stack blocks and knock them down. This helps with coordination and grasping.

64. Treasure Hunts: Treasure hunts are an excellent way to build motor skills. Prepare a list of items and matching clues to help them out when searching.

65. Dancing and Moving to Music: Put on some fun children's music and move together. Dancing improves balance, sense of rhythm, and flexibility.

66. Playing with Shape Sorters: These toys help toddlers learn how to manipulate objects and fit them into the proper spaces. Great for developing fine motor control and hand-eye coordination.

The goal is to keep them active and engaged. Combining structured activities with free, self-directed play allows toddlers to strengthen their bodies and build new skills at their own pace.

Safety Tips and Guidelines

When your children are playing, there are some safety precautions to keep in mind:

- **Adult Supervision:** You always want to keep an eye on your child during these activities, especially if your toddlers are between the ages of 1 and 3.

- **Age-Appropriate Materials:** Make sure that the materials you use in the activities are age-appropriate and safe for your child.

- **Safe Play Environment:** Work hard to create a safe play environment for your toddler by removing potential hazards or obstacles. Secure cords, keep electrical outlets covered and ensure all the furniture or play equipment is stable and secure. If you are outdoors, do the same, and make the area free from harmful objects or substances.

- **Hygiene and Cleanliness:** Maintain your child's hygiene and cleanliness during sensory activities involving food, water, or sensory bins. Their hands and materials must be clean to prevent the spread of germs.

- **Allergies and Sensitivities:** Be aware of any allergies or sensitivities your child may have, especially when engaging in activities involving food, materials, or outdoor environments. Be careful and avoid allergens or irritants that may cause harm or discomfort to your toddler.

Remember, these safety tips are general guidelines, and assessing the specific activity and environment is essential to ensure the child's safety.

15 Easy Exercises for Toddlers

Below are more exciting activities for you and your toddler to keep things fresh and fun! These activities can be played both indoors and outdoors:

67. **Water Play:** Use tubs, buckets, and other containers to splash and pour water.

68. **Musical Instruments:** Musical instruments like shakers, drums, and xylophones will allow your toddler to experiment and develop their creativity.

69. **Sensory Art:** Help them explore textures and materials like playing with playdough or paints.

70. **DIY Sensory Bottles:** If you are looking for an excellent way to stimulate your child's visual and auditory senses, creating sensory bottles using water, glitter, small toys, beads, etc. is a good way!

71. **Balloon Play:** Engage in activities like balloon volleyball.

72. **Pretend Play:** By encouraging imaginative play with pretend kitchens, doctor kits, or dollhouses, you get to build your child's creative imagination.

73. **DIY Instruments:** Help them create simple instruments using household items like rice-filled bottles or rubber band guitars.

74. **Indoor Camping:** Set up a cozy blanket fort, read books, or play with flashlights.

75. **Sorting Games:** Improve your child's senses by using objects like colored blocks or shapes and sort by color, size, or shape.

76. **Bean Bag Toss:** Create targets using hula hoops or buckets and make it a fun game by having them toss bean bags into them.

77. **DIY Sensory Board:** Make a sensory board with different textures, buttons, zippers, and Velcro for exploration.

78. **Outdoor Nature Art:** Create beautiful natural outdoor artwork by using items like leaves and flowers.

79. **Color Scavenger Hunt:** Take scavenger hunting up a notch by helping them find objects of different colors around the house or outdoors.

80. **Play With Scarves:** Give them colorful scarves for them to wave, throw, and catch.

81. **Water Sponge Play:** Give them sponges and a bucket of water for squeezing and soaking up water. This simple process will keep your toddler engrossed and fascinated.

With these engaging exercises, toddlers can build their physical abilities through interactive play. Parents should supervise activities and provide guidance to keep things fun and avoid frustration. Starting simple and progressing as skills improve will help your toddler gain confidence in their movements and balance over time. Keep mixing the activities between energetic and calm, indoor and outdoor. The key is to make physical activity a fun and regular part of your toddler's day. Now get out there and play! Your toddler will thank you for it, and you'll both get to build great memories of your time together.

Chapter 5: Reading and Acting

Kids are naturally creative, curious, and imaginative. They like to think outside of the box and explore their surroundings. They are also very sensitive to their environment. Everything they observe, hear, or come into contact with leaves a mark of some kind. Acting and reading activities will allow your child to view others and the world differently. Improv offers a creative outlet for self-expression and serves as a safe and fun learning experience.

Reading with your toddler can improve their reading and language skills.

The activities in this chapter will improve your child's reading and language abilities and expose them to the beauty of acting and performance. These exercises will work wonders for their confidence and motor skills as well. This chapter delves into the magical effects of story-telling, reading, and acting on a child's imagination, creativity, and understanding. Doing these activities with your child is a surefire way to foster their love for books and the world of theater.

Benefits of Reading and Acting

Reading and acting skills can improve your child's social skills and teach them to interact with others. Improv teaches children to look for shared interests with people, search for creative and interesting conversation openers, and unleash their imagination. Understanding how to make friends and build relationships from a young age will set them up for success later in life.

Interactive reading, acting, and improv incorporate physical activities that encourage children to coordinate their brains, eyes, and movements, which improve their motor skills and increase their self-reliance. Reading new books, creating stories, using props, and learning lines will also expand your child's vocabulary and teach them to learn new tools. This might help them develop reading and writing skills sooner.

You should also consider trying these exercises with large groups of people to improve your child's confidence. Acting, self-expression, and public speaking will teach your child to be comfortable in front of a large crowd. This skill will benefit them significantly in professional and academic settings.

Teaching your child to think in new and unconventional ways will make their lives easier as adults. Complex problems require creative solutions, and there is no better way to improve their problem-solving skills than through reading and improv. These activities expose your child to a wide array of scenarios that will encourage them to express themselves and work their way innovatively through challenges. Since most of the activities in this chapter require at least two people, they will also learn the importance of teamwork and understand how to work effectively with others to achieve the best results.

The following improv and reading exercises will test your child's creativity and imagination while enhancing their emotional intelligence, comprehension skills, empathy, attention to detail, and self-confidence. You can do these exercises alone with your child, but they're much more fun when done in groups. Most of these games can be enjoyed by adults as well. You can get the entire family involved!

82. Use Unconventional Props

In this improv game, your child should use any object around the room to create a skit. Encourage them to use the item in an unconventional way other than its intended use. This exercise aims to get your child to channel their creative thinking skills to be as unexpected and funny as possible. For instance, they might use a kitchen bowl as a hat or a shoe as a smartphone.

83. Character Impersonation

This challenges children's contemplation, analysis, and application skills. They need to consider all the characteristics of the character that they'll impersonate, from tone and expression to appearance and behavior, to integrate them into their performance. Cut up small pieces of paper, writing the name of a movie or cartoon character that your child knows on each one. Remember that the characters you choose must have distinctive and unique characteristics.

Place the pieces of paper into a bowl and ask your child to draw a name. Anyone who isn't playing can assist the child with reading the character's name. The other players will have to guess the character based on their impersonation. For instance, if they received Cinderella, they can integrate a broom, toy birds, or slippers into their performance.

84. Animal Impersonation

This exercise is designed to get children to think about body language and non-verbal communication. Even though this can be challenging for a toddler, they'll try to figure out how an animal's movements and behaviors can capture its essence.

Ask your child to choose an animal and keep the choice to themselves. They should then try to mimic the animal's behavior for other players to guess. Make sure to take turns so your child gets a chance at guessing. Guessing encourages them to work on their interpretation, inferential, and attention skills.

85. Group Story-Making

Making a story in pairs or as a group requires anyone involved to use their collaboration, creativity, and listening skills. The game begins with the first player saying the story's opening line. The following person then says another logical line to the story. The players keep taking turns, building on the narrative until the story ends. Work together to make the story as coherent and enjoyable as possible, incorporating a problem and resolution to the narrative. You can write each line down or use your phone to record the game to read the final result out loud when you're done.

86. Make Assumptions

This will encourage your child to explore their imagination and read body language. If done often enough, it can help them develop a sense of empathy. They'll also learn that there are always untold stories and reasons behind people's actions and behaviors. Observe passers-by whenever you and your child are out, and start making assumptions about them.

Think about where they came from, where they're going, what they like doing in their free time, what they do for a living, and whether they have a family. Observe their facial expressions and body language, creating background stories for them. For example, if you see a woman in formal attire with a frown, you might assume she got demoted or fired. Remember to keep your voices lowered so you don't accidentally offend someone.

87. Choose Someone to Imitate

If your child has a favorite actor, search for one of their scenes on YouTube and show it to them. Experiment with ways to imitate their body language, tone, emotions, and voice together. If they don't have an actor in mind, watch a movie together. When you're done, have them choose their favorite character. You can also choose yours so you can both recreate your favorite scenes. You don't need to copy everything they do. However, you should try to get them to focus on the details, like mannerisms, how they talk, and even their walk. That is the whole purpose of the exercise.

Impersonation makes anything more fun.
Scott Barlow, (CC BY-NC-ND 2.0) <https://creativecommons.org/licenses/by-nc-nd/2.0/>
https://www.flickr.com/photos/barl0w/2983543259

88. Copying Roles

This exercise will get your child thinking about how different people act based on their roles. It will also enhance their emotional awareness over time. Each profession requires a different tone of voice, range of emotions, body language, and energy. Your child will try to copy three roles they're familiar with; for example, teacher, police officer, and scientist. Set a timer, asking them to improvise for 30 to 40 seconds before shifting to the next one.

89. Simplified Pictionary

While Pictionary is best played in groups, you can play it alone with your child. Write simple words on pieces of paper and put them in a bowl. Ask someone who isn't playing to assist your child with reading the term when it's their turn. They will then draw a word for you to guess what it is. Take turns, giving your child the opportunity to guess.

PICTIONARY WORDS

Shoe	Fish	Rooster	Egg
Door	Sandwich	Dress	Bird
Trash Can	Cookie	Aeroplane	Octopus
Christmas Tree	Socks	Bubbles	Star
Television	Book	Ocean	Coffee
Moon	Pants	Ball	Apple
Eyes	Happy	Banana	Mailbox
Spider	Roof	Butterfly	Nose
Snow	Candy	Cupcake	Tree
Drum	Skateboard	Rainbow	Cat
Shirt	Sun	Grapes	Leg
Sad	Water	Pizza	Lips
Doll	Bed	House	Cloud
Cup	Hat	Sleep	Orange

90. Interactive Movement Books

Interactive movement books can improve a child's motor and comprehension skills. Read books that incorporate physical activity and are suitable for your child's age. Opt for books that encourage children to move around and use positional concepts. This way, when the text says, "on the table," your child can point to or touch the surface of a table.

If the book incorporates action words, such as "run, "clap," or "jump," your toddler can do these actions. For example, if the book mentions the color red, you can ask them to quickly find something red in the room. Get as creative as possible to engage your toddler in the story-telling process.

91. Set a Word Limit

Ask your child to think of a concept or object they can explain in 1 to 10 words. For example, if they think of the moon, they can say round, sky, night, and shine. Take turns so both of you can get a chance to explain and guess.

92. Use the Last Letter

Play a word game where you can only say one word, starting with the last letter of the word the other player used. To make the game more educational, you can set a theme for the exercise that aligns with the concepts that your child is learning in preschool. If they're learning about countries, for example, you can go: "France," "Egypt," "Tanzania," etc.

93. Get Moving

This is one of the easiest and most fun improv exercises toddlers can do. It requires no verbal communication, making it suitable for children who can't yet think on their feet. One person can call out pairs of things, such as lock and key, for the other to depict them using only their body.

94. Mimic the Emotions

This game can improve a child's emotional awareness and cultivate their sense of empathy. Initiate a conversation with your child, expressing several emotions throughout. If you show excitement, your child should attempt to portray that emotion and copy your body language as if staring at a mirror. Their emotions and facial expressions should shift as you shift to anger, sadness, or a neutral expression.

95. Space Jump

This fun exercise will test your child's reactivity and critical thinking skills. Ask your child to act out any scene they desire. You should then shout "space jump" whenever you want them to freeze in place. The second player should get into the first player's frozen position (your child, in that case) before starting their scene. The whole point here is to freeze as soon as the words "space jump" are said while thinking of a very challenging position to baffle the other player.

96. Consider the Environment

This is yet another non-verbal improv game that will get your child's creative juices flowing. One player should secretly think of a setting and act how they would if they were actually there. For instance, they must act frightened yet excited if they're pretending to be at a theme park or pretend they're shopping if they think of the mall. The player must think of a tricky setting to make it harder for others to guess.

Improv and reading games can offer many benefits and entertainment for children and adults alike. These exercises will not only strengthen your bond with your child, but they'll also strengthen your language, communication, critical thinking, and problem-solving skills. Reading and improv exercises will teach your child much about others and the world around them, allowing them to cultivate a more profound sense of understanding, acceptance, and empathy.

Chapter 6: Exploring Nature

Nature is the finest teacher your toddler can ever have. It is one of the oldest forms of sensory-motor development for children. After all, before the birth of civilization, only nature existed in its raw, unrestrained glory. Apart from sensory motor skills, your child can learn and experience the science of exploring, the art of paying attention, the thrill of taking risks, and develop fine and gross motor skills. With every new thing they learn, their confidence will grow, and their social skills will improve. Needless to say, they will acquire several physical skills along the way.

More importantly, your toddler will learn to appreciate nature. Today, when computers and smartphones are ruling people's waking hours and exciting new gadgets are being invented every week, affinity and love for nature are rapidly declining. How often do you stand and feel the grass beneath your feet, stop and smell the flowers strewn in your front yard, or wait to observe a caterpillar transform into a butterfly?

Since your child will develop a love for nature at a very young age, the bond will stay with them for years ahead. And when they grow up, you might just find them going to explore the great outdoors from time to time!

Ideally, you can leave your toddler to crawl or run free on your lawn or in a nearby park. They will develop all the skills above on their own. But the best way to go about it will be with the aid of outdoor activities. It is more fun and educational, and you can also become a part of their sensory growth regime. Here are a few exciting ways of exploring nature with your toddler.

Collecting rocks with your toddler can be a form of sensory play.

Your toddler's curiosity will lead them to touch every new thing they see. And the most prominent things that they see in nature are rocks, leaves, and twigs. These come in many shapes, colors, sizes, and textures. Two major senses come into action here: sight and touch.

Start off small. Show them how to grasp a rock and bring it to you. Then, ask them to bring another rock and then another. Let them observe its texture and feel its form. Is it circular? Let them feel its shape. Show them other similarly shaped rocks and ask them to bring you more. Progress to the color of the rock. Is it black? Ask them to bring more black-colored rocks.

Understanding textures may be slightly more difficult for them. But texture contrast won't be hard to grasp once they can differentiate between colors and shapes. You can conduct a similar activity with leaves and twigs. Encourage them to keep a collection of these things, then show them how to sort them according to shapes, sizes, colors, and textures.

98. Color Scavenger Hunt

Now that they can understand the difference between various shapes, sizes, colors, and textures, you can progress to a slightly more difficult yet interesting activity: a scavenger hunt. Perceiving different colors is one of the easiest things for toddlers; thankfully, nature is ripe with objects of various colors. All you need is an item list.

Start with the primary colors: red, green, and blue. Your child will be effortlessly able to distinguish between these. Here's how you can prepare for the hunt.

1. Draw three squares, one below the other, on a plain white piece of paper.

2. Fill the first square with green (easiest to find in nature), the second with red, and the third with blue.

3. Show them how to bring a green-colored leaf and place it on the green square and red and blue colored fruit/flower on the respective squares.

4. Ask them to do the same on their own.

Over time, you can move on to other colors found in nature.

99. Universal Scavenger Hunt

Expand your item list to other things found in nature. Draw a leaf, rock, twig, butterfly, worm, flower, fruit, etc. You can't expect your child to bring every little thing on their own (butterflies are tough to catch!), so help out wherever necessary.

Scavenger hunts improve your toddler's observation and memory retention. Plus, it is much more fun to match colors, shapes, objects, etc., in nature than merely on a piece of paper.

100. The Natural Sandbox

You don't need a special sandbox when you can give your child a natural one. Take them to the beach, or let them dig up garden soil. Provide an incentive by hiding small toys like squishy ducks and slinkies beneath the surface. Digging not only strengthens their palms but also stimulates their sense of touch.

101. Wet and Dry Sorting

Another basic way to improve your child's touch sense is to make them understand the difference between wet and dry. Take them to a nearby lake and place two boxes of different colors (say black and white) in front of them. Pick up a wet pebble and place it in their hand, then ask them to drop it in the black box. Place a dry pebble in their hand to drop into the white box. Let them repeat this exercise by themselves and behold the joy on their face when both boxes are filled!

102. Smelling Flowers and Tasting Fruits

Tasting fruits can introduce toddlers to new food items.

This is an upgraded version of the scavenger hunt. Once your child can match the pictures of fruits and flowers in a book to the actual object, you can have them smell the flowers and taste the fruits. Now, keeping the picture book open, hide the flowers and fruits. Remove one petal from each flower and chop a tiny part of each fruit. Ask them to smell the flower or taste the fruit and have them point out the right flower or fruit in the picture book.

Start with only two flowers or two fruits at first. They may get it wrong a few times, but as their senses of smell and taste get used to the activity, they will get it right eventually.

103. Playdough in Nature

Textures are often hard to memorize by touch alone, not just for children but for adults, too. That is where modeling dough comes in. Ask your child to press different kinds of rocks in the dough. That way, they can see the texture while feeling it with their hand, making it easier to memorize. Then, you can play a scavenger hunt with them using textures as clues!

104. Snow or Mud Creations

Making a snowman with your toddler can teach them different shapes.

It is fun for toddlers to play in the snow or mud. But it is even more exciting for them to create stuff with snow or mud. It's a natural version of playdough. Start with simple things. Show them how to create a ball. Progress to a snowman or mudman, followed by basic shapes like mountains and walls. Let their imagination run wild after that.

105. Nature Art

So far, your little one may have drawn random shapes on paper or created paint impressions of indoor objects. It's time to take their creativity outside. Let them play with crayons or paint on a blank paper while sitting in your backyard. You may notice a difference in their indoor scrawls and outdoor ones. The latter may be slightly more artistic. That is their imagination!

Alternatively, you can make your child do impressions of leaves and flowers on a blank canvas. Let them dunk it in paint and slap it on the canvas, and watch them smile in delight!

106. Tree or Rock Painting

Why limit your toddler's creativity to a piece of blank paper? Take them back to the Stone Age and let their art bloom on the bark of a tree or a large rock. Keep those crayons and brushes aside. All they need is paint and their hands. The existing textures or colors on the tree or rock will add to their imagination, boosting their creativity.

107. Garden Assistant

Kids often mimic what their parents do. If you take your child along while tending to your lawn, they will likely mimic what you do. For instance, after watching you pull out weeds a few times, they will eventually start tugging on the grass themselves. They probably won't have enough strength to pull it out yet, but it's the act that matters. It shows that they are excited to assist you in your gardening chores. So the next time around, give them the tools for the job, like a toy watering can.

108. Dancing in the Rain

Back in the day, your parents may have warned you about playing in the rain. But you may have gone ahead and jumped and splashed around anyway; it was a lot of fun, wasn't it? Let your child experience that fun, too. Recent studies have shown that the benefits of playing in the rain far outweigh its drawbacks. Your child develops gross motor skills, thus learning how to be careful in wet weather at a very young age. Other benefits include increased immunity, peaked sensory skills, and improved physical skills.

109. Feeding Birds

Birds are nature's gift to humankind. But it's hard for children to watch birds up close. Their restlessness and quick movements often drive the birds away. Teach your little one how to make the birds come to them. Teach them how to feed those feathered creatures. They are generally hungry for sunflower seeds. Keep a bowl of it in your yard, and let your child watch as the birds flock together for a feast.

110. Walking Barefoot on Grass

It's best to let your child roam around in nature barefoot. It is probably the easiest kind of sensory play on this list. A few minutes of barefoot walking will start building the muscles of their feet, gradually enhancing their overall balance while walking or running. And, of course, the feel of grass, dirt, and pebbles will heighten their sense of touch.

111. Cloud/Star Gazing

Is your toddler tired of doing all the activities mentioned so far? Many of them can be exhausting. This is the perfect time to let them lie down on the cool turf and stare at passing clouds or the twinkling stars. Use your imagination to form different shapes with the clouds and describe your visualization to your child. Rock shapes are easiest to visualize, and their developing imagination can connect with the shapes they most recently played with.

Before you head out with your little one to explore nature, there are a few precautions you need to take. Make sure to clear the area of any rocks with jagged edges or pieces of glass. Scour the vicinity for bees or other harmful insects. Most importantly, don't let your child out of your sight, especially if you are in a public park.

Chapter 7: Having Fun in the Kitchen

You don't have to wait for your children to join school to start learning about science when you can easily do that at home. The kitchen is one of the best places you can teach your toddler about basic science. Even something as simple as melting chocolate can be a learning experience for your child and an opportunity for you to spend time with them. You can do various activities like cooking, baking, experimenting, or trying out sensory activities with your little one. The creative opportunities in a kitchen are endless, and the best thing about these activities is that you probably have all the supplies you need already in the kitchen.

Toddlers can learn about science in the kitchen.
https://www.pexels.com/photo/mother-and-child-in-the-kitchen-5082625/

In addition to science experiments, your child can partake in simple cooking rituals to help with their cognitive development. In fact, cooking is considered a STEM activity, and toddlers are completely capable of cooking with basic utensils, some simple appliances, and your supervision. These activities will save time, keep your child occupied, and help them learn basic concepts like following instructions, measuring, mixing, counting, etc. More than anything, children love to help you in the kitchen. Sure, they tend to make a mess, but with the right activities, it will be worth it.

Kitchen Experiments

112. Milk Swirl Experiment (Ages 3-11)

This simple science experiment is safe for children of all ages and super interesting, especially for toddlers. Plus, you'll find all the ingredients in your kitchen. The end result is a beautiful explosion of colors that leaves toddlers – and even you – in awe.

Materials:

- Food coloring
- Whole milk
- Dishwashing soap
- A plate or bowl
- A jar or cup
- A cotton swab

Instructions:

1. Gather all the materials and place them on the kitchen counter where your child can see them.
2. Have your child pour some milk into the plate or bowl.
3. Ask your child to pour one drop of each food coloring right into the center of the milk.
4. In a jar or cup, take some of the liquid dishwashing soap. Dip the cotton swab into the soap until the end is immersed.
5. Finally, give your child the cotton swab and ask them to touch it gently to the food coloring drops in the milk.
6. Enjoy the final explosion of colors!

113. Fizzing Colors (Ages 3-12)

This is another colorful kitchen experiment that is simple to execute and can catch your toddler's attention. Plus, you only need three simple ingredients for this experiment.

Materials:

- Food coloring
- 1 cup baking soda
- ½ cup white vinegar
- A baking sheet or pie pan
- An eye dropper or pipette

Instructions:

1. Gather your ingredients and arrange them on the kitchen counter.
2. Put an even layer of baking soda on the baking sheet or pie pan, covering the surface uniformly.
3. Hand your child the food coloring bottles and ask them to pour drops all over the baking soda. Make sure they don't squeeze out excessive quantities of the color solutions.
4. Take some of the white vinegar and drop it in using the eye dropper, pipette, or even a straw.

5. Voila! You'll see an explosion of colors full of bubbles.

114. Instant Sensory Snow (Ages 3-8)

If your toddler loves to play with snow, this activity is perfect for them. It creates instant snow for sensory play; although it's fake, the snow will feel real to them. The best part? All it takes is three simple steps.

Materials:

- ¼ cup White colored shampoo
- ½ cup Baking soda
- Measuring cup
- Tray

Instructions:

1. Cover the tray with the baking soda.
2. Add the shampoo to the top of the baking soda.
3. Ask your child to use their hands to mix these two ingredients together. After a while, the mixture will take on a less crumbly and sticky mixture and start to resemble the texture of real snow.

115. Sink or Float? (Ages 3-8)

This simple activity will teach your toddler about the concept of sink and float. This experiment is fun for children of every age but especially helpful for toddlers.

Materials:

- A large container for water
- Two containers
- Small toys

Instructions:

1. Ask your child to gather all their toys for a fun activity.
2. Label the two containers: "sink" and "float."
3. Fill up the large container with water.
4. Explain the concept of floating and sinking to your child, and then ask them to drop their toys into the water container one by one.
5. If the toy floats, put it into the float container. If it sinks, it goes into the other container.
6. Halfway through the activity, start making predictions about whether the toy will sink or float to make the activity more fun.

116. Marshmallow Slime (Ages 3-10)

Slime is all the rage among children of all ages. But instead of getting your child one of those toxic chemical slimes, what if you could make edible slime with marshmallows? Of course, this doesn't mean they should be encouraged to eat this, but only that it's safe for young children.

Materials:

- Food coloring
- Powdered sugar
- Measuring cups
- Bowl and spoon
- Marshmallow fluff

Instructions:

1. Transfer the marshmallow fluff to a bowl, and add the food coloring to the mix.
2. Next, place the powdered sugar on a clean surface and place the now-colored marshmallow fluff on top of it.
3. Knead the mixture until your desired consistency is achieved.

117. Edible Structures

This activity introduces the concepts of engineering and construction to children while combining yummy snacks in the process. It's very easy to set up and uses supplies already available in your kitchen.

Materials:

- Toothpicks
- Apple slices
- Marshmallows
- Cheese blocks (small)
- Crackers

Instructions:

1. Ask your child to build a structure using the toothpicks and the snacks by stabbing the toothpick into the snack.
2. You can create towers, tall structures, horizontal shapes, or any kind of geometric shape as long as the structure remains stable.
3. Tell your child they can have all the snacks they use to make their structure.

118. Grow Salt Crystals

This fun activity for growing salt crystals will keep your child's curiosity and attention for a while. It's a safe experiment that can be performed with a toddler and uses just a few simple ingredients.

Materials:

- Water
- Construction paper
- Salt
- Tray
- Container
- Pencil, scissors, and hole puncher

- A string

Instructions:

1. Cut a small shape from construction paper and punch a hole near the top.
2. Tie a string through the hole and hang the shape inside the container.
3. Pour water into the tray and place the container in the center.
4. Sprinkle salt evenly into the container.
5. Let it sit undisturbed in a warm area to allow crystals to form.
6. Check regularly, and remove the shape when crystals form.
7. Let the crystals dry completely.

119. Dancing Raisins

Is this science? Magic? This activity helps children learn about the states of matter, densities, and simple science. Sounds tough, right? It's actually easier than it sounds.

Materials:

- Glass
- Raisins
- Club soda

Instructions:

1. Pour the club soda into the glass until it's a quarter filled.
2. Ask your child to add some raisins to the glass.
3. Observe as the raisins go to the bottom of the glass, then float to the top and back to the bottom again, as science works its magic.

Tasty Recipes

120. Garden Salad

If you want to get your child to eat healthy, have them make a garden salad with you. They might not be interested in eating it if you make it, so ensure they're involved. Have them chop the lettuce and add the ingredients together.

Ingredients:

- 1 to 2 tbsp of ranch dressing
- 2 to 4 tbsp of diced cooked chicken
- 1 cup lettuce, sweet corn, diced tomatoes, diced cucumbers

Instructions:

1. In a large bowl, ask your child to add the ingredients one by one.
2. Once added, you can season the salad with salt, pepper, and ranch dressing.
3. Mix the salad with two spoons or forks, and have your child follow your lead.

121. Banana Bread

This toddler-friendly recipe is not only delicious but also easy to follow. Your toddler can even do all the steps themselves if you guide them through the process.

Ingredients:

- ½ plain flour
- 2 bananas
- 1 ½ self-rising flour
- ½ cup brown sugar
- ½ cup milk
- 2 eggs
- 50g of butter
- Cinnamon

Instructions:

1. Before you can start preparing the bread, preheat the oven to 180 degrees Celsius
2. Combine all of the ingredients in a large container and mix them thoroughly
3. Mash the bananas in a bowl, then add the butter, milk, and eggs.
4. Add this mixture to the large container, and then transfer it into a greased loaf pan
5. Put this in the oven for about 45 minutes until it's done.

122. Quesadillas

Quesadillas are the perfect snack! This easy recipe will help your toddler learn how to make simple quesadillas, and once they get the hang of it, you can add more ingredients to the basic recipe.

Ingredients:

- 4 tortillas - medium-sized
- 2 cups of shredded cheese (Mozzarella, Cheddar)
- Fillings - as desired (shredded chicken, green bell peppers, sliced onions, mushrooms, diced tomatoes, cilantro, spinach, sweet corn, etc.)

Instructions:

1. Coat a large pan or griddle with olive oil and heat it at medium-high for two minutes before adding the tortilla.
2. Let it warm for about 30 seconds, and then add cheese to one side of the tortilla.
3. Once the cheese is a little melted, add the rest of the ingredients, fold the tortilla, and press.
4. Before flipping the tortilla, cook for about five minutes and press using a spatula.

123. Quiche

This simple recipe is perfect for toddlers to learn about stirring and mixing food. You can have your child crack eggs and beat them to make this yummy veggie quiche.

Ingredients:

- 1 pie dough
- 3 to 4 slices of bacon
- 1 cup cheese (Swiss)
- 5 large eggs
- 1 ½ cups of mixed vegetables (bell peppers, yellow onion, mushrooms, broccoli)
- ½ tsp salt
- White pepper

Instructions:

1. Preheat the oven to 375 degrees. Roll out the dough into a pie plate and set it up. Place it into the fridge to cool.
2. Cook the bacon over medium heat until it browns. Once done, remove the bacon, but keep the pan on the stove.
3. Now, add the vegetables to the pan one by one and cook for a few minutes.
4. Whip up the eggs, salt, and pepper in a separate bowl.
5. Add the egg mixture, bacon, and vegetables to the pie plate, half at a time. Make two layers until the pan is filled up.
6. Place it into the oven and let it bake for 30 minutes.

124. Vegetable Soup

Vegetable soup is relatively easier to make than most food items and will teach your children how to measure the ingredients. Having them cut the veggies with a safe knife will also help develop their skills.

Ingredients:

- Salt and pepper
- Chopped spring onions
- Corn flour
- Sweet corn
- Chopped coriander leaves
- Milk

Instructions:

1. Cook the tender corn separately in a pressure cooker.
2. Blend the remaining corn with half of the milk and salt to create a smooth paste. Strain the mixture.
3. Transfer the mixture to a pan and cook on low heat. Add milk and coriander, then boil it on medium heat for five minutes.
4. Dissolve the corn flour in the remaining milk, mix well, and add it to the pan along with the seasoning.
5. Garnish with spring onions.

125. Sandwiches

Helping your child learn the basic skill of making a sandwich at an early age is a favor to both of you. All they have to do is gather the ingredients and place them on the bread. It doesn't even involve fire or a knife.

Ingredients:

- 1 large / 2 small slices of cooked chicken breast
- Lettuce
- Tomato
- 3 slices whole meal bread
- 1 tbsp hummus
- Cucumber
- Carrot

Instructions:

1. Toast the bread and cut off the crusts if you feel like it. Totally optional!
2. Grab a vegetable peeler and shred the cucumber and carrot into thin strips.
3. Slather some yummy hummus on all three slices of bread.
4. Take one slice and pile on the lettuce and juicy chicken breast.
5. Add another slice of bread and load it up with tomato, cucumber, and carrot.
6. Finally, pop that last slice of toasted bread on top, and you're good to go!

126. Grilled Cheese

This is every child's favorite meal. This simple recipe makes it the best choice for parents and children alike.

Ingredients:

- Bread
- Cheese
- Mashed Sweet Potato
- Butter

Instructions:

1. Take one piece of toast and spread the sweet potato on it. On another piece, add the cheese.
2. Melt some butter in a pan and then place the bread with the fillings facing up. Swirl it around a bit to coat the bread with butter. Cook until the undersides of both slices are nicely toasted.
3. Put the two slices of bread together and press down gently.
4. Cut it up, and it's ready to be served. Enjoy!

Participating in the kitchen doesn't just have to be an adult's job. Having your child help with cooking – and even the simple science experiments mentioned in this chapter – will help improve their cognitive development significantly. Plus, you'll get to spend time with your little one while doing your chores!

Chapter 8: Developing Cognition

During toddlerhood, children undergo an intense phase of cognitive development, allowing their minds to process and organize information more effectively. This encourages them to learn about their environment, improve their language acquisition skills, and develop avenues for self-expression. Consequently, the cognition-boosting activities geared toward toddlers must be engaging and adaptable to the children's individual needs and personalities.

This chapter delves into activities specifically designed to boost cognitive development in toddlers. These exercises aim to improve problem-solving abilities, memory, and logical thinking. On top of that, the different games and activities are not just educational but also fun, cultivating a positive attitude toward learning and thinking.

127. Memory Game with Flashcards

Using pairs of picture cards for a simple memory game will powerfully affect your child's cognitive development. Flashcard games improve concentration and memory skills. Start with simple shapes, colors, nature, and literary or math concepts like animals, letters, and numbers. Make it a daily practice to show them 1-2 flashcards (at first; later, you can increase the amount) and have them memorize the contents to stimulate their minds.

red 

green 

blue 

orange 

yellow 

pink 

gray 

purple 

red 

green 

blue 

orange 

yellow 

pink 

gray 

purple 

128. Close-Ended Games

Close-ended games foster children's cognitive development by promoting their problem-solving skills. Activities most recommended for close-ended learning involve pegs and peg boards, mazes, gears, and stacking rings. However, you can use any toys, activities, or items that encourage your child to be persistent in completing a task. No matter how hard they have worked to succeed, the sense of gratification they experience later builds up their confidence and motivates them to engage in new cognition-developing experiences.

Here's an example of a close-ended activity, stacking rings:

1. Get your toddler to sit on a mat and place the ring dowel in front of them.
2. First, slowly stack the rings yourself.
3. Start removing the rings one by one and examining them in front of your child.
4. Show that you can put your hand through the ring or look through it, and encourage the child to do the same.
5. Once they understand that the hole in the middle allows the rings to be stacked on the dowel, tell your child about the different sizes.
6. Explain that the rings can only be stacked in a specific order, which depends on their size.
7. Show this to your child by placing the largest ring on the dowel, followed by the next one in size. Finish up with the smallest ring.
8. Have them try stacking the rings by themselves. If they make a mistake, explain what this means. For example, if they try to put on the smallest ring first, they won't be able to do this because of its size.

129. Color Sorter Activities

Color sorters are great for teaching young toddlers about the fun world of colors. As your child explores the different colors, they become more and more interested in memorizing and recalling the colors of different objects around them. Buy or make a color sorter for your child to boost their logic and reasoning skills.

Here is how to make a DIY color sorter:

1. Get colored paper in 3-4 different colors and items to sort. For younger children, these should be small toys (preferably uniform ones that come in different colors).
2. Tape the papers onto the ground and put down a handful of toys.
3. Ask your child to sort the toys by color.
4. If needed, offer suggestions like, "You need to match the toy with the paper." or "The red toy goes on top of the red paper, the yellow to the yellow paper..."

130. Learning about Cause and Effect

Toys with buttons to push are great for teaching your toddler about cause and effect. Understanding this phenomenon is fundamental for healthy cognitive development in children. It can be as simple as using a toy that makes a sound or lights up when your child pushes a button. They will have tons of fun and learn that every action has an effect.

131. Stacking Wooden Blocks

Stacking wooden blocks is probably one of the most well-tried activities for enhancing cognitive development in young children. It's relatively simple, and you'll only need wooden blocks of various sizes and colors. Encourage them to stack the toys any way they want to foster creativity. As they do, they use their imagination, develop logic and memory skills, and more. If needed, offer some suggestions for making a particular shape.

132. Exploring Textures through Touch and Feel

Your toddler probably has tons of toys with different shapes and materials. So why not put random toys in a box for a texture exploration activity? They will enjoy sorting through them and hone plenty of cognitive functions in the process. Like in many other facets of children's development, sensory activities like touching and exploring different textures play an enormous role in cognitive development. You can incorporate this exercise into activities like playing outdoors, exploring nature, or getting familiar with arts and crafts. For example, letting your child explore the different textures of playdough and other craft materials will encourage them to consider how to use them. They learn how the different materials feel separately and together to decide whether it's a good idea to combine them or not. If you have an older toddler, let them decide what items they want to explore - but make sure they're age-appropriate and don't represent a choking hazard.

133. Hiding Objects

Finding hidden objects makes children use several cognitive processes, including logic, reasoning, and visual and short-term memory.

Instructions:

1. Show your toddler a small toy (something you can hide between your palms) and ask them to take a good look at it.
2. Then, ask them to look away and close your hands over the toy.
3. Lastly, ask your toddler what toys are between your hands.
4. Once your child has mastered the previous step, you can step it up by hiding objects under a blanket or towel. Make sure it's an item they're familiar with.
5. Have them look for the object. They'll have to recall what the items look like as they can't see it directly.
6. You can then start hiding objects in other easily accessible places to foster your child's desire for exploration and discovery. Both of these are fundamental for cognitive development.

134. Setting Up Simple Daily Routines

Setting up simple yet consistent routines for your child isn't only beneficial for laying a foundation for the scheduled activities they'll be required to partake in once they start kindergarten and school, but it's also great for enhancing their cognitive abilities like logic and reasoning. Learning about routines encourages children to develop the ability to follow instructions. From ages two and up, toddlers can understand when it's time to eat, get dressed, take a bath, tell stories, go to a park, and play. If these activities come in a sequence, they'll always know what comes next and learn to expect it. Routines foster a sense of discipline and normalcy, which contributes to balanced development. The best way to get your child to adhere to routines is to give them choices while teaching the specific task-time relation. For example, before snack time, let them choose between two options. Or, let them choose which toy they want to play with during bath time. Nurturing their drive for independence is just as crucial for your toddler's cognitive development as is adherence to routines.

135. Sorting-Based Toys and Games

Older toddlers can identify toys and small household objects and sort them. You can Create a homemade shape sorter with a cardboard box and colored shapes to get your toddler to recognize and categorize different shapes. You can start by asking them to sort blocks or toys based on color, shape, or size. Then, you can incorporate sorting games into their schedule, like meal or bath time. For example, you can give your toddlers different measuring cups and let them play with them in the bathtub. Then, ask them to use the largest one to scoop water over a bath toy. They will have to figure out which one they should use. 2-3-year-olds can be asked to help sort household items.

136. Encourage Letter and Number Learning

Letters and numbers are the basic tenets for learning pre-literacy language and math skills, so it's a good idea to familiarize your child with these as early as they can grasp this concept. There are numerous ways to teach toddlers numbers and letters - from teaching counting and alphabet songs to encouraging them to use magnets and blocks depicting letters and numbers. For older toddlers acquainted with the names of household items, you can cut out letters and stick them to the objects whose names begin with that letter. Look for opportunities to count objects with your toddler whenever possible throughout the day.

137. Organizing and Recognizing Toys and Household Objects

Toddlers can learn a lot from classifying objects. For younger toddlers, focus on teaching them how to organize toys and other objects by shape and color. Once they've mastered this, you can ask them to arrange colored blocks, pegs, and other items from large to small. The next step is to encourage them to pick out items of a specific color or shape. Then, take it a step further and ask your toddler to pick out other household items (like the smallest cup, a blanket of a specific color, etc.) as you go with them about their daily routines.

138. Age-Appropriate Puzzles

Introducing simple jigsaw puzzles to encourage problem-solving skills and persistence is a great way to improve your child's logic and reasoning skills. Age-appropriate puzzles for toddlers come in all shapes and sizes - from interactive animal puzzles to 2D or 3D puzzles for spatial play. The latter usually has smaller pieces the child needs to fit together to create a larger object. During this, they learn how to work out how the smaller pieces can come together in space through trial and error. Likewise, interactive animal puzzles require children to match the sounds of the animals with their pictures. Whichever type of puzzle you get, make sure to start with a small number of pieces. For younger toddlers (12-18 months), this is around 2-4 pieces, while older children (20 months and older) can match up to 10 pieces. Your child must be able to visually identify the parts so they can use their logic and memory to complete the puzzle.

Here is a quick guide for helping your toddler master puzzles (if they haven't already):

1. Put the puzzle piece in front of your toddler and encourage them to put the pieces together.
2. Let them lead by letting them figure out the logical orientation of the different pieces. It will make them more interested in the activity - and, consequently, learn more.

3. Following your child's lead, you'll learn about their interest and provide further tools for their cognitive development. You'll also be able to notice if they get stuck in finding the specific position of the puzzle pieces.

4. If your child has difficulty with this activity, ask them to think about how to solve the problem (for ages 2 and up) or offer solutions (for 1-2-year-olds). For example, you can ask them to look closer and determine where else a specific piece fits or suggest that they turn it the other way.

5. When your toddler gets it right and completes the puzzle, praise them for their effort to boost their confidence and encourage them to tackle new problems.

139. Gathering Objects

Gathering objects is an open-ended activity that encourages children to explore and manipulate the world around them. Through it, your child can learn all about the items they explore and acquire new skills. For example, while gathering objects, they'll see that different items can be used in multiple ways. Likewise, they become more persistent in finding specific things and can even learn simple math and science concepts. They develop their reasoning skills and learn by example as they interact with you or whoever is helping them gather the object.

To encourage this cognition-boosting opportunity, make a list of objects you want your toddler to find, then have them explore, collect, manipulate, and experiment with the items. Some ideas for gathering items are muffin pans, cups, funnels, small bottles or jugs, plastic utensils and lids, small mirrors, pieces of fabric, tubes, and other household items.

140. DIY Toddler Puzzles

Helping your toddler create their own puzzle improves cognitive development. You can help them make simple but interactive puzzles - or, if they have an older sibling to help them, even better. Either way, it can be a wonderful bonding activity for children and parents.

Instructions:

1. Have your child paint or draw a picture - or you or an older sibling can do this instead if your toddler is too little for this.

2. Cut the picture into four or more pieces (depending on the child's age - the younger they are, the fewer pieces they can match).

3. Encourage your child to put the picture back together by arranging the "puzzle" pieces in the appropriate order and placement. This will make them use and develop their problem-solving skills.

141. Matching Post-It Shapes

Matching Post-its is another marvelous way to introduce toddlers to shapes, colors, numbers, letters, and other concepts. If you don't have a ready-made activity on hand, you can always make one from Post-it notes. Here is how to do it:

1. Get sticky notes in different colors. Cut little shapes like squares, hearts, circles, rectangles, and triangles from each color. Keep the stick part when cutting.

2. Cut the exact shapes you made from sticky notes from colored cardstock, just a little bigger.

3. Place double-sided tape on the wall or table and attach the cardstock cutouts.

4. Arrange the small shapes under them and have your child match the sticky shapes to the corresponding bigger ones by attaching them to the right place.

5. You can coordinate colors, too, depending on your toddler's abilities.

6. Encourage your child to choose the corresponding shapes themselves, but step in to help if they are stuck.

Chapter 9: Fostering Social Strength

Social development is vital in shaping children's abilities to interact, communicate, and collaborate effectively with others. Engaging in activities that enhance interaction, sharing, empathy, and cooperative play can be an excellent way to promote these essential social skills while making learning enjoyable and engaging.

Promoting social skills is important for toddlers.

Enhancing Interaction

One key element of social development is encouraging interaction capabilities in your child. Promoting your children to engage in conversations, educating them on the benefits of active listening, and letting them understand the necessity of non-verbal communication will let them create stronger social connections. Interactive activities like team-building exercises, group discussions, and collaborative projects can help children boost their communication skills. These activities will also foster a sense of mutual understanding and let them build better connections with their peers.

Promoting Sharing

Making your child understand the necessity of sharing is an awesome social strength to develop. The focus of sharing here is to share beyond material possessions, like sharing experiences, ideas, and emotions. Encouraging your child to share their interests, thoughts, and ideas promotes a sense of being connected. Community service projects, group storytelling events, and team exercises are excellent platforms to let your child share their perspective and stay motivated through the supportive and collaborative environment.

Developing Empathy

Empathy is one of the foundation pillars of social strength, which enables the child to understand and respect the feelings of others. When your child develops empathy, it promotes the development of healthy relationships with their peers, allows them to resolve conflicts, and helps them understand how to adequately address the people around them while respecting their emotional state. These activities help children better understand diverse perspectives, cultivate compassion, and strengthen their emotional intelligence, ultimately nurturing their ability to connect with others on a deeper level.

Encouraging Cooperative Play

Co-op play encourages your child to work together with other children toward achieving a common goal. The activity promotes problem-solving skills, letting your child understand teamwork and cooperation. Cooperative games, group challenges, and related projects should be encouraged in your child as those allow them to experience sharing, the necessity of communication, and to develop better negotiation skills. Co-op play will also let your child understand the significance of pursuing a common goal over individual success and recognize the value of teamwork in certain situations. They will eventually develop strong social bonds with their peers.

As parents, fostering social strength in children is crucial for their overall development and future success. Engaging children in play activities that promote interaction, sharing, empathy, and cooperative play helps them develop essential social skills and makes the learning process enjoyable and engaging. By providing opportunities for children to interact, share, empathize, and collaborate, you empower them to navigate the complexities of the modern world, build strong relationships, and become confident and empathetic individuals.

Fostering Social Strength through Play Activities

142. Turn-Taking Games:

Instructions:

1. Gather children and introduce them to turn-based games like "Pass the Ball" or "Duck Duck Goose."
2. Give the ball to a child and instruct them to pass it to the child on their right.
3. Encourage them to wait patiently for their turn and let the ball be passed down to them.

In "Duck Duck Goose," children sit in a circle, and one child goes around tapping others on the head, saying "duck." When they say "goose," the tapped child gets up and chases the first child around the circle, trying to tag them before they reach the vacant spot.

Duck Duck Goose.
Jon Fleshman, CC BY 2.0 DEED <https://creativecommons.org/licenses/by/2.0/>
https://flickr.com/photos/louisvilleusace/5740729000/

Benefits:

Turn-taking games promote sharing, patience, and cooperation. Children learn to wait for their turn, respect others' opportunities, and practice social skills in a playful environment.

143. Puppet Show:

Instructions:

1. Provide children with finger puppets and encourage them to create a puppet show.
2. You can provide a scenario the children can enact, letting their imaginations run wild.
3. Now, encourage each child to express their feelings and participate in the puppet show.
4. Instruct the children to take turns, switch finger puppets with other children, and interact with each other through these finger puppets.

Benefits:

Enacting a puppet show fosters social strength by developing better communication skills and letting children express their opinions, emotions, and creativity through storytelling.

144. Building Blocks:

Instructions:

1. Provide building blocks or construction toys to the children.

2. Encourage them to work together to build structures.

3. Children can take turns adding blocks, sharing ideas, and collaborating on building different structures like towers, houses, or bridges.

Benefits:

This activity promotes collaboration, teamwork, and creativity in your children as they understand the benefits of working together, respecting the opinions of others, and learning to work together on a common goal while sharing the available resources.

Building blocks encourage creativity
https://pxhere.com/en/photo/499153

145. Arts and Crafts:

Instructions:

1. Gather art supplies like crayons, markers, chart papers, scissors, and related tools.

2. Introduce children to the art station, explaining about the activity.

3. They can pick the desired art supplies and craft the art projects they like.

4. Instruct the children to collaborate, share their art supplies with other children, and create a collaborative art project.

Benefits:

Collaborative art projects foster cooperation, communication, and creativity. Children learn to share materials, negotiate ideas, and appreciate each other's contributions.

146. Role-Playing:

Instructions:

1. Provide costumes or props, or encourage children to use their imagination to act out different roles.
2. They can pretend to be characters like doctors, teachers, or animals and engage in imaginative play scenarios.
3. Have them take turns playing different roles and interacting with each other.

Benefits:

Role-playing activities enhance social skills, empathy, and creative thinking. Children learn to understand different perspectives, practice communication, and develop cooperation through collaborative play.

147. Storytelling:

Instructions:

1. Provide picture books or story cards with illustrations.
2. Children can take turns telling stories based on the pictures or cards provided.
3. Encourage them to use their imagination and create a story together, each contributing to different parts or taking turns adding elements to the narrative.

Benefits:

Storytelling activities promote listening skills, turn-taking, and imagination. Children develop language skills, creativity, and cooperative storytelling abilities.

148. Cooperative Board Games:

Instructions:

1. Choose cooperative board games such as Snakes and Ladders or Pandemic.
2. Gather children around the game board and explain the rules.
3. Emphasize that the goal is to work together as a team to achieve a common objective.
4. Encourage them to discuss strategies, make joint decisions, and take turns playing the game.

Benefits:

Cooperative board games foster teamwork, problem-solving, and sharing. Children learn to collaborate, communicate, and support each other while enjoying the game.

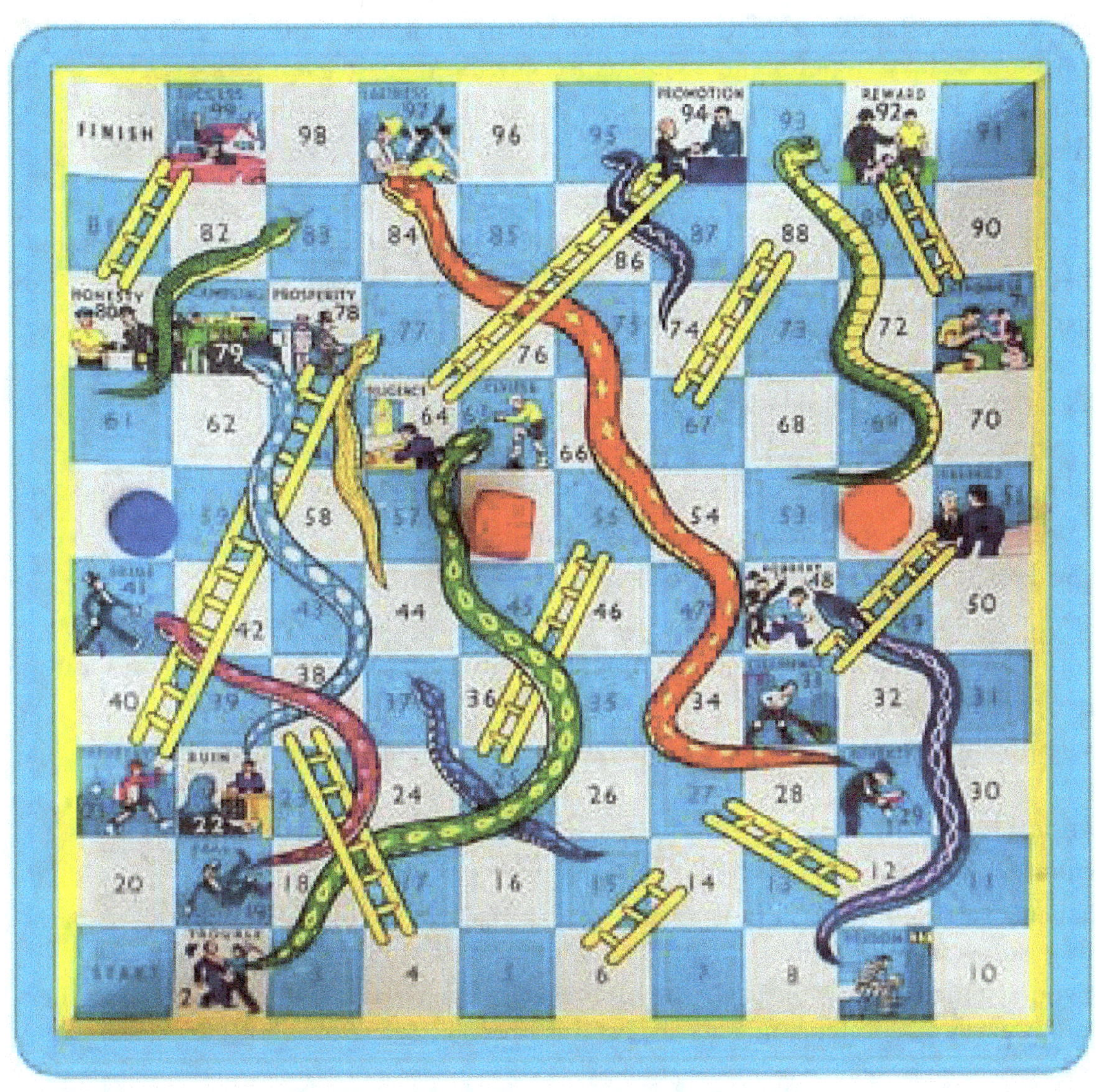

Snakes and Ladders is a fun cooperative board game for children and adults.
Leonard J Matthews, CC BY-NC-SA 2.0 DEED <https://creativecommons.org/licenses/by-nc-sa/2.0/>
https://www.flickr.com/photos/mythoto/9720925815

149. Outdoor Scavenger Hunt:

Instructions:

1. Create a scavenger hunt list with specific items for children to find in nature or their surroundings.

2. Divide children into teams or pairs and provide them with bags or baskets to collect the items.

3. Encourage them to work together, communicate, and help each other find the items on the list.

Benefits:

Outdoor scavenger hunts promote cooperation, communication, and observation skills. Children learn to collaborate, share responsibilities, and appreciate the value of teamwork.

150. Group Art Project:

Instructions:

1. Provide a large canvas or poster board and art supplies.
2. Children can collaboratively create a large artwork by taking turns adding their own touches.
3. Encourage them to discuss ideas, share materials, and work together to complete the artwork.

Benefits:

Group art projects encourage teamwork, communication, and creativity. Children learn to respect others' ideas, share resources, and contribute to a shared artistic vision.

151. Cooking or Baking Together:

Instructions:

1. Choose a simple recipe and involve children in preparing it.
2. Provide them with age-appropriate tasks and utensils.
3. Encourage them to take turns measuring ingredients, stirring, or decorating.
4. Emphasize the importance of cooperation, following instructions, and sharing responsibilities.

Benefits:

Cooking or baking together promotes cooperation, following instructions, and sharing. Children learn to work together, practice basic culinary skills, and enjoy the fruits of their collective efforts.

152. Musical Jam Session:

Instructions:

1. Gather a variety of musical instruments, real or makeshift, and invite children to participate in a music jam session.
2. Encourage them to take turns playing instruments, singing, or creating rhythms together. Promote communication, cooperation, and respect for each other's contributions.

Benefits:

Musical jam sessions foster creativity, cooperation, and turn-taking. Children learn to listen, communicate, and collaborate while expressing themselves through music.

153. Sensory Play:

Instructions:

1. Set up a sensory play station with materials like sand, water, or playdough.
2. Encourage children to explore and play together, taking turns and sharing sensory experiences.
3. Provide tools and molds for them to use and engage in cooperative sensory play.

Benefits:

Sensory play activities promote cooperation, sharing, and sensory development. Children learn to communicate, negotiate, and engage in collaborative sensory experiences.

154. Building a Fort:

Instructions:

1. Provide blankets, pillows, and chairs to create a fort or a cozy reading nook.
2. Encourage children to work together, plan the structure, and construct the fort.
3. They can take turns arranging the materials, suggesting ideas, and creating a comfortable space to enjoy.

Benefits:

Building forts promotes teamwork, problem-solving, and imaginative play. Children learn to cooperate, communicate, and collaborate in creating a shared space.

155. Group Dance or Movement Activity:

Instructions:

1. Play upbeat music and encourage children to dance or engage in movement activities together.
2. Promote group dances or simple choreographed movements that require coordination and cooperation.
3. Encourage them to take turns leading or suggesting dance moves.

Benefits:

Group dance or movement activities foster coordination, cooperation, and self-expression. Children learn to follow instructions, cooperate with others, and express themselves creatively.

156. Cooperative Sports:

Instructions:

1. Choose cooperative sports games such as relay races or group challenges.
2. Divide children into teams and explain the rules.
3. Encourage them to work together, communicate, and support each other to achieve the common goal.
4. Emphasize the importance of taking turns, sharing responsibilities, and celebrating collective achievements.

Benefits:

Cooperative sports activities promote teamwork, communication, and physical coordination. Children learn to collaborate, strategize, and appreciate the value of collective effort in sportsmanship.

Fostering teamwork within toddlers and developing social and interpersonal skills are necessary for their overall growth and development. By engaging in activities that promote collaboration and cooperation, toddlers learn valuable skills that lay the foundation for their social interactions and relationships later in life.

Teamwork encourages toddlers to work together towards a common goal, whether building a block tower, completing a puzzle, or participating in a group activity. Through these experiences, they understand the importance of sharing responsibilities, coordinating efforts, and relying on others. By working as a team, toddlers learn to communicate effectively, listen to others' ideas, and respect diverse perspectives.

Developing social and interpersonal skills is essential for toddlers to navigate social situations and build positive relationships. By engaging in collaborative activities, toddlers learn how to take turns, share resources, and resolve conflicts peacefully. They develop empathy and learn to understand and respect the emotions and feelings of others. These skills help them to interact with their peers in a considerate and inclusive manner, fostering harmonious social dynamics and reducing instances of conflict.

Teamwork and social interaction also contribute to developing important cognitive and emotional skills. Toddlers learn problem-solving abilities as they negotiate and find solutions collectively. They develop patience as they learn to wait for their turn and understand that everyone's contributions are valuable. Through collaborative play, they gain a sense of belonging, self-confidence, and a positive self-image as they realize that their ideas and efforts matter within the group.

Furthermore, teamwork and social development provide a solid foundation for future academic success. By learning to work effectively in groups, toddlers develop skills such as active listening, cooperation, and effective communication that are vital for collaborative learning environments. These skills will continue to benefit them as they progress through school, higher education, and later in their careers.

Fostering teamwork within toddlers and developing their social and interpersonal skills are crucial aspects of their overall development. By engaging in collaborative activities, toddlers learn the value of working together, communicating effectively, and respecting others. These skills provide a strong foundation for building positive relationships, navigating social situations, and succeeding academically and professionally later in life.

Chapter 10: Quiet Time and Its Endless Possibilities

Quiet time is an essential part of the day for toddlers, as it gives them a chance to take a break from some of the more stimulating activities of the day and relax for a while. This part of the day involves them playing quietly and on their own, so it also gives parents some time away from the toddlers. This alone time proves to be quite nurturing for young children, as it helps them become more independent, relaxed, and confident. When done daily, this part of the day reduces the frequency of your child's tantrums and meltdowns. Plus, you don't need hundreds of toys to make quiet time fun for your children. And don't even think about handing them a screen. All you need are open-ended activities that allow your child to use their creativity and imagination but are also low-key enough that they do not require supervision. This chapter includes several fun activities that you can include in your toddler's quiet time.

157. Coloring Activities

Coloring has a certain appeal to children, especially young toddlers. The activity of coloring can reduce stress and promote relaxation in children and even adults! It can also help with the development of their fine motor skills.

Materials:

- Colors
- Markers
- Crayons
- Coloring book
- Coloring pages
- Blank pages

Instructions:

1. You can either get your toddler a simple coloring book or print some coloring pages for them.
2. Alternatively, you can give them blank sheets to draw and color on.
3. Show them how to hold a colored pencil, marker, or crayon and how the color should be filled in.
4. Try not to limit their creativity by having them draw or color a specific way, and just let them do their own thing.

158. Building Toys

Building toys are among the most common activities children are engaged in during quiet time. Whether you get them large building blocks or tiny Lego sets, they will stay creatively engaged in the process while their fine motor abilities develop.

Materials:

- Building blocks or Lego sets
- Clean and safe play area

Instructions:

1. Set up a clean and safe play area.
2. Choose age-appropriate building blocks or Lego sets.
3. Show your toddler how to stack blocks or connect Lego pieces.
4. Let them use their creativity to build their own structures.
5. Offer guidance and support as needed.
6. Allow free playtime.
7. Clean up together after playtime.

159. Puzzles

Puzzles are interesting to children.

Puzzles are intriguing for young children, especially once you show them how they're done. To keep them engaged, you'll have to make sure the puzzle sets you get are neither too difficult nor too easy. Getting puzzles with colored pieces will be an added bonus to catch your child's attention. It's best to start with big, chunky pieces and then work your way to more complex ones.

Materials:

- Puzzles
- Play area

Instructions:

1. Show your child how to solve a simple puzzle to help them understand the process.
2. Encourage your child to observe the patterns and colors on the puzzle pieces.
3. Guide them in placing the pieces in their correct positions, only offering assistance when needed.
4. Support their problem-solving skills and celebrate each time they're successful.
5. Allow your child to work on the puzzles independently, and be there just in case they need help.
6. If you're using a puzzle with small pieces, you must watch your child closely to ensure they don't swallow a piece.

160. Pretend Play

Pretend play is something all children love to do. Their imagination works wonders for them, and they get to spend time alone. Whether your toddler likes to play doctor, house, or any other pretend scenario, all you need to do is give them the right props and some directions.

Materials:

- Play props and costumes

- Pretend play sets or accessories (e.g., kitchen set)

- Decorative elements (e.g., mini-furniture)

- Open-ended props (e.g., a blanket to make a fort)

- Printed or handmade visual aids (e.g., pretend money)

Instructions:

1. Ask your toddler what they would like to play with today. They'll probably have a favorite, like a teacher, doctor, or chef.

2. Gather the props, toys, or costumes they can use in their chosen scenario. For instance, if they want to play a doctor, get them their toy doctor set.

3. Set up a play area in their room where they can freely engage in this activity.

4. Let your child take the lead and start the scenario. Don't try to restrict their imagination by telling them to be rational.

5. Participate in the pretend play by taking on supporting roles, like being the patient in their doctor scenario.

161. Audiobooks

If you don't want your children to spend time looking at a screen, another way to keep them engaged and entertained is to put on audiobooks. There are numerous stories with engaging audiobooks that spark creativity and will be very interesting for your little one. This will also help with their literacy development, and they can learn valuable lessons along the way.

Materials:

- Audiobooks or audio story recordings

- Device or audio player

- Comfortable listening area or headphones

Instructions:

1. Choose stories that are age-appropriate for your child. For toddlers, some great books to start with are:
   - "Goodnight Moon" by Margaret Wise Brown
   - "The Very Hungry Caterpillar" by Eric Carle
   - "Brown Bear, Brown Bear, What Do You See?" by Bill Martin Jr. and Eric Carle
   - "Guess How Much I Love You" by Sam McBratney
   - "Where the Wild Things Are" by Maurice Sendak
   - "Corduroy" by Don Freeman
   - "Dear Zoo" by Rod Campbell
   - "The Cat in the Hat" by Dr. Seuss

2. Ask your child which story they want to listen to, and play the audio at a suitable volume.

3. Encourage your child to listen actively and let their imagination run wild.

4. After the story, ask your child about the lessons they learned.

162. Dry-Erase Activity Board

Get a whiteboard, also known as a dry-erase activity board, for your toddler to keep them engaged during quiet time. This will also help their educational learning, as they can practice their numbers and letters on it. They can even use colorful markers to make illustrations without making a mess of things.

Materials:

- Dry-Erase Activity Board (with built-in markers and erasers or separate markers and erasers)
- Dry-erase markers (non-toxic and washable)
- Soft cloth or tissue for erasing

Instructions:

1. Introduce the board and markers to your child, and explain how they can use them.

2. You can start by having them trace letters, numbers, shapes, or drawings to help their hand get steady.

3. Encourage them to be creative and explore different colors and drawings.

4. Make sure they don't try to ingest the markers or write on the walls when you're not looking.

163. Button Trees

This fun quiet time activity is an engaging task that will offer your child lots of learning opportunities. You'll have to create a colorful tree using pipe cleaners, and your child can thread buttons onto the tree branches. This will improve their creativity and enhance their hand-to-eye coordination.

Materials:

- Pipe cleaners in various colors
- Buttons in different sizes and colors
- Small container

Instructions:

1. Take a pipe cleaner of your chosen color and fold it in half to create the tree trunk.

2. Twist the folded end of the pipe cleaner a few times to secure the trunk shape.

3. Bend the rest of the pipe cleaner to form branches, leaving some space at the end for attaching buttons.

4. Ask your child to thread buttons into each branch one at a time.

5. You can ask them to first thread buttons of a specific color or size, then follow with the rest.

6. Have them count the buttons as they thread them into the tree branches.

7. Ensure you keep an eye on your child while playing with the buttons to prevent them from ingesting one.

164. Crazy Straws

For this fun, quiet time activity, you'll first have to craft the crazy straws sequence and then have your child play with the different shapes, colors, and sizes. You can have them sort colors, sizes, and shapes or even create a rainbow!

Materials:

- A few crazy straws
- Felt in different colors

Instructions:

1. Cut different shapes out of the felt. You can do circles, squares, triangles, hearts, and stars.
2. Punch a hole in the center of these shapes, big enough to fit the end of a straw.
3. Mix the shapes together and place them in a container. Place the straws on a surface, and ask your child to thread each shape into the crazy straws one by one.
4. Either instruct them to make a specific pattern or have them do it themselves.

165. Chalkboard Table

Reuse an old table and blackboard to make the perfect drawing space for your toddler. This may sound complicated, but you need to follow just a few steps to make one. Your child will love playing with different colored chalks and being able to scribble on a table.

Materials:

- An old table
- Paint roller
- Chalkboard paint
- Chalks

Instructions:

1. Clean the surface of the table you're using, and start painting the top with blackboard paint.
2. If you don't have a paint roller, you can always use a paintbrush, but remember it will take longer. Let the table dry.
3. After a few hours, paint a second coat over the dried paint and leave it to dry overnight.
4. Once it's done, test the surface by rubbing the side of the chalk onto the surface and rubbing it off with a board rubber.
5. Give your child some toddler and let them get creative.

166. Matching Objects

These simple toddler puzzles need little to no crafting or preparation and will keep your child engaged for a while.

Materials:

- Markers
- Cardstock
- Toys
- Scissors

Instructions:

1. Cut the cardstock in half.

2. Use the markers to trace your child's toys onto the cardstock. You can have your child choose their favorite toys and trace those yourself.

3. If your child knows how to trace, ask them to trace their toys themselves.

4. Now, mix up the toys, lay out the puzzle pieces, and have your toddler match each toy with its outline.

167. Calm Down Jar

Calm-down jars are a must-have if you have toddlers, especially if it's hard to get them to quiet down. These are also called mindfulness jars because their beautiful and glittering swirling patterns keep your child's attention.

Materials:

- Plastic bottles or jars
- Hot water
- Mixing bowl
- Whisk
- Liquid watercolor or food coloring
- Fine glitter
- Glue

Instructions:

1. Put some hot water in the mixing bowl, and add the clear glue to it. Mix thoroughly.

2. Add the watercolor, food color, and glitter into the mix, and whisk it again.

3. Once everything is blended completely, pour the mixture into the plastic bottle.

4. Mix one last time before transferring the mixture into the bottle to avoid leaving any glitter behind.

5. Shake the bottle vigorously and hand it to your child.

168. Action Figures and Dolls

Playing with action figures and dolls is a wonderful opportunity for children to engage in imaginative and creative play. With a collection of action figures or dolls and related accessories, toddlers bring their characters to life, create stories, and embark on exciting adventures.

Materials:

- Action figures or dolls
- Accessories or props

Instructions:

1. Gather action figures or dolls along with their accessories.

2. Encourage your child to create stories and scenarios with the figures/dolls.

3. Provide a designated play area or playmat for their playtime.

4. Let them dress up the figures/dolls and set up props for different scenes.

169. Latch Board

A latch board is a fun activity that aims to improve young children's fine motor abilities. It has all sorts of latches, hooks, locks, and keys. Playing with a latch board will keep your toddler engaged during quiet time, and this activity doesn't require you to supervise them.

Materials:

- Latch board (pre-made or DIY)
- Clean and safe play area

Instructions:

1. Get a latch board of appropriate difficulty for your child. This activity's purpose is to teach your toddler independence.
2. Introduce the board to your child and show them how to use the different hooks, keys, and latches.
3. Encourage your toddler to explore the latch board independently, allowing them to manipulate the latches and learn how they work.
4. Let them practice their fine motor skills by opening and closing the different mechanisms on the board.

170. Feed the Monster Game

This fun game is a fine motor skills development activity that can keep your child engaged. You'll have to turn an old empty tub of wipes into a monster and use pom poms, buttons, and other small items as food.

Materials:

- Empty box of wipes
- Craft supplies (construction paper, googly eyes, markers, glue)
- Pom poms, buttons, or other small items as "food"

Instructions:

1. Turn the empty box of wipes into a monster face using construction paper, googly eyes, markers, and glue.
2. Cut a mouth shape large enough to put small items in.
3. Scatter pom poms, buttons, or small items around the tub as "food."
4. Encourage your child to pick up the small items and feed them into the monster's mouth.
5. Support their fine motor skills and hand-eye coordination during play.
6. Celebrate each successful "feeding" and offer rewards or points.

171. Calming Yoga

Yoga can help your child wind down.

Calming yoga is the perfect quiet-time activity if your little one has a hard time winding down for a nap. This activity provides a constructive outlet for all their unused energy and makes them tired enough to go to sleep. So, teach your child some basic yoga poses and practice them with your child at the end of their quiet time activities. You can even give them some simple yoga cards with visual cues to practice all the poses on their own.

Conclusion

Toddlers experience a better sense of self-confidence when they can put their creativity to use. They feel great when they realize they can create something with minimal assistance. They also feel proud of themselves when they receive positive feedback and reactions to something they've created. Showing a child that their artwork is valued will encourage them to continue working on their skills.

Children are met with various choices and conflicting ideas when they explore their creativity and spontaneous thoughts. Having to choose between certain color or pattern combinations, images to draw or color, and materials to use encourages them to make decisions and solve problems. Creative activities allow children to think outside the box and trust their judgment. Having fun is also important for a child's well-being, as it offers a break from routines, rules, and expectations. Creative activities offer a safe space for children where experimentation, mistakes, and expression are encouraged.

Now that you've read this book, you know how to channel your child's creativity into fruitful experiences. You know the go-to activities to do with your child whenever they need to work on their cognitive, sensory, physical, emotional, or social skills. The majority of a child's education happens at home. That's mainly because they have more space and freedom of expression there. Unfortunately, traditional educational systems suppress children's imaginative and creative tendencies. They turn down alternative ways of thinking and solving problems. The activities offered in this book will allow you to make the most of your child's time at home, ensuring healthy and enriching brain development.

Your home activities can bring your attention to their hidden talents and hobbies. Your child will never know if they like cooking, gardening, or beading if they never try it. This book might be why you discover your child is a skilled actor or singer. Applying the information you learned here will teach you a lot about yourself and your child.

Parents, caregivers, and babysitters can benefit from the activities in this book. Besides connecting and spending quality time with the toddler, creative play aids neural connectivity in the brain's frontal lobe during adolescence and early adulthood. The part of the brain that develops last is responsible for planning, sound decision-making, and prioritizing. Having fun with a toddler also allows you to get in touch with your inner child and unwind from the responsibilities and stressors of everyday life.

Part 2: Play Therapy Activities for Toddlers

101 Fun Games and Exercises to Enhance Motor Skills, Emotional Regulation, and Problem-Solving Abilities While Strengthening Your Bond

Introduction

Have you ever been amazed by how dynamic your toddler is? One second, they're a bundle of laughs. The next, they're a storm of tears. There's so much potential within that tiny personality of theirs. As their parent or caregiver, you have made an excellent decision to look into the magic of play therapy. Using this tool, you can become a pro at understanding the big feelings in your little child and help them become a more independent person confident in themselves. You'll learn how to be your child's rock so you can guide them on their journey to adulthood with love.

This book was specifically written for parents worried about their child's development. It's for caregivers who want to help the tots in their care to get better at self-expression. It's also been written for therapists and teachers who want to know how best to work with toddlers to give them the hang of their emotions and understand the world around them. It contains therapeutic activities to help toddlers become the best version of themselves as they grow and develop.

To make this book easy to use, all the processes described here are written in a simple and easy-to-understand way. You will see the importance of play in helping your toddler naturally express themselves clearly and confidently. Discover a treasure trove of creative ideas for your toddler to play their way to a full and rich life. Everything in the following chapters will facilitate your toddler's physical, mental, social, and emotional development.

Chapter 1: The Magic of Play

If you could peek into your little one's mind, you'd be amazed at what goes on in there. It's sad that many people don't pay as much attention to their children's minds as they do everything else. You must consider your child's mental health as seriously as you do their body, and there's no better way to help them process their emotions than through play therapy. So, what does this mean? Do you just let your child go out to play? Is that it? Then, after that, do you send your children to therapy to lie down on a couch? What exactly is play therapy, and how do you use it to help children?

What Is Play Therapy?

Your toddler's mind is full of creativity, imagination, and wonder. The best way to interact with it is through the language of play. When you do that, you get to understand what your child thinks, how they feel, and what their experience in life is like. Play therapy is the gateway that allows you to enter into this world of imagination and creativity. It allows your child to express what goes in their head in a way you can understand and appreciate.

Play therapy allows your toddlers to express themselves.

Play therapy is all about letting your child fully express themselves. They deserve to explore how they feel in order to be able to understand their experiences. If you attempt to ask a child things an adult would be better at answering, you cannot expect them to respond clearly. Your child may also feel uncomfortable as they struggle with the complex concepts you present and ask them to unravel. Play therapy is a better alternative as this is a non-intrusive way to gently coax them into revealing their inner thoughts and workings. Play is the language of children. Children live in a make-believe world where imagination is not contained or constrained.

The Purpose and Benefits of Play Therapy

Your child stands to benefit a lot from play therapy. It places them in a world carefully created to allow them to play without any constraints. In this sort of environment, your child feels safe. They can wildly and freely release their innate creativity and dive deeper into their inner world. To understand play therapy's benefits, you must take a holistic look at your child's life. Think about your child as a four-part being: physical, emotional, cognitive, and social.

Play therapy allows your toddler to express themselves physically in a way that contributes to developing their gross and fine motor skills. Gross motor skills are necessary for the proper functioning of the entire body. They are responsible for standing, running, walking, sitting, jumping, kicking, lifting, etc. Fine motor skills like writing, threading a needle, and tying shoelaces require precision and control. With play therapy, your toddler will learn how to coordinate their hand movements with the visual information their eyes and brain offer them. They'll become aware of their body, the space around it, and how to move confidently through it. They'll also learn how to use their hands to write, draw, hold things, etc. They must partake in play because this is how they encourage the connections in their brain. This way, they can also develop confidence when it comes to interacting with the environment around them.

Now, onto their emotional health. Play therapy lets your toddler express all feelings and emotions, whether negative or positive, in a safe space. It allows them to externalize all their emotions so they can effectively process them. When working with play therapy to encourage emotional expression, it could involve creating a story, setting up a challenging event for your toddler to figure out, or using role play where they can feel like they are in charge. They get to feel like they have the power to explore their emotions and process them effectively. When they have the chance to express their feelings using the language of play, they become emotionally resilient and better able to handle the ups and downs that inevitably come with life.

Next, consider your toddler's cognitive health. Play therapy is an excellent tool to encourage them to develop their intellect. Engaging with their imagination and setting up scenarios where they have to solve problems or make decisions allows them to cognitively thrive. This indirectly encourages them to have flexible thinking, to come up with their own unique ideas, and to reason their way through any situation or scenario in which they might find themselves.

With play therapy, you'll also be improving your child's memory and language skills. You encourage them to tell stories as they chat freely with the therapist while getting them to think about the possible meanings of the stories they create. By working with these cognitive processes, you'll find your toddler increases their mental capacity. This makes it so they have an excellent starting point for all intellectual and academic goals they have in the future.

Finally, consider your toddler's social ability. If you want them to learn how to interact with others, they've got to develop interpersonal skills. Play is the perfect tool to help them learn the social norms and rules of etiquette that guide interactions in society. As they play, they grow confident in their ability to connect with others and maintain the relationships they find. Face it: Relationships are complicated and require more flexibility in thinking and emotional intelligence than a child may have. Therefore, engaging your child in play therapy makes it easier for them to understand what relationships are all about. They'll figure out when to negotiate, when to cooperate, and when to recognize that they're dealing with a difficult individual. You can have your child participate in group therapy or cooperative play with other children to learn the importance of sharing, waiting their turn, and respecting other people's boundaries. In this situation, you create a microcosm of society for your child to explore and understand. By doing this, you help them realize who they are, how to regulate their emotions, and how to connect with others healthily while respecting their personal boundaries and those of others as well. For these reasons and many more, play therapy is absolutely essential for your child. It is essentially a form of therapy that uses play to help your child discover and deal with psychological, emotional, and social challenges.

Real-Life Applications of Play Therapy

Play therapy can help your child deal with difficult emotions. For instance, imagine that your 5-year-old has lost their pet. It's tough for them to understand that they will never see it again. Death, as a concept, doesn't make much sense to your child, and loss is a heavy burden to bear. Engaging your child in play therapy makes it easier for them to learn the skills necessary to calm and ground themselves to heal. You can give your child a small toy representing the pet to make things easier. You can even recreate situations that remind them of the fun that they had with their pet. This might seem like a way to conjure up bad emotions, but it will offer your child a form of catharsis and teach them how to honor those they lose. They can learn to safely express grief and allow themselves to process the trauma of loss, all while holding on to the memories of their pet.

Next, imagine that your daughter has trouble integrating with others in kindergarten because she feels deep anxiety that holds her back from connecting. With play therapy, you can set up a situation for her to learn what it means to safely interact with others. Scenarios meant to explore the ideas of conflict, conflict resolution, friendship, and so on can be set up to teach her the intricacies of interacting with others from a place of kindness and empathy. These skills are necessary for her to learn so she can manage her social life and become confident enough to interact with anyone. She'll learn that the rejection of others is not a reflection of who she is.

Imagine another situation where you have a child dealing with trauma, perhaps one resulting from abuse by previous caregivers. With play therapy, you encourage these children to come out of their shells and to get in touch with what they need. The therapist guides the child to tell their story in a comfortable way while giving voice to all the ugliness within. For instance, the therapist may offer the child colors, paint brushes, and a blank canvas, encouraging them to use the art supplies and express what they feel inside. Usually, the work created by the child is an accurate reflection of their feelings, and not only that, but it also serves as an outlet for the traumatic pain that they deal with on the inside. The more your child is encouraged to express themselves in this way, the better they will deal with the trauma and pain. After this, they can move on to healing and becoming whole, healthy beings.

Building Empathy and the Parent/Caregiver-Child Bond

Using play therapy, it is possible to encourage a stronger, better connection between a child and their parent or caregiver. First, play therapy allows your child to exist in an environment that is safe and supportive of who they are. It's a pity that most children cannot simply be themselves. Sometimes, parents have the wrong idea of good parenting; other times, these children live in abusive, unsafe environments. With play therapy, the therapist works to keep your child in a playroom filled with all sorts of art supplies, toys, and anything else that makes it fun and safe for your child to fully and freely express themselves. This will offer your child a much-needed sense of security, which is essential for successfully navigating life as an adult. Also, having them feel safe and secure will make them feel much better about opening up to you because they now understand that they can create this feeling within themselves and not have anyone else take it from them. As your child plays in this environment, you are welcome to observe and even participate when you feel it's right. That will give you a unique perspective on your child's world and how you can better interact with them.

Secondly, play therapy is also essential for building trust between you and your child. Mentally healthy people can empathize with others. It's the ability to understand what someone else is going through that makes it possible to cultivate trust in all relationships. Trust and empathy are irrevocably linked. Trust lets you connect with your tots and understand them better. So, during play therapy, the therapist acts as a trusted figure and uses active listening empathy to get through to your child.

It's easy for your child to trust the therapist because the environment in which they will be playing is deliberately crafted to elicit a sense of safety. Also, play therapy involves being well attuned to everything about the child, from the words they say to the actions they take, as well as the things that remain unspoken. In this environment, your child understands that it is fine to express everything they feel because they know they will not be judged. They learn to let go of the self-consciousness that keeps them trapped in their own heads. By mirroring what the play therapist does with your child, you can also create this bond with them. You can teach your child that you are to be trusted, and they will eventually open up to you. This will further enhance the connection you will share.

By allowing children to express how they feel using play, you teach them that it is safe to be their emotional selves. Unfortunately, in certain families, children are not allowed to fully express their emotions because often, the adults in their lives are not comfortable with the truth. However, by using play therapy, you teach your child that their emotions are valid and should be expressed fully and freely.

The final point to consider when working to enhance the bond between your child and yourself is that the language of symbolism is a major tool in play therapy. It is an excellent way to uncover the truths that your little one carries within, which would unlock their personality and give you a clear understanding of who you're dealing with. Your therapist has been trained to deduce your child's various experiences, how they feel, and how they perceive the world. The more your child works with these symbols, usually dolls and toys, the more you will find yourself understanding how they process things.

Symbolic play involves the representation of actual situations in life that your child may have experienced or will experience. It gives them the chance to handle that situation in a safe space. Using this, you can show them that there's always a way to face those situations, no matter how impossible it may seem. You can use a doll to represent someone they care about, like a parent, a friend, or even themselves. Doing this gives them the emotional distance required to process what they're feeling and express it freely. You can observe their choices, the stories they lean towards, and how they react emotionally as they engage in this symbolic play to get to know them better.

Play therapy is an excellent way to discover your child. The more you learn about them, the more empathy you have for them. Also, children are incredibly perceptive. The fact that you're taking the time to understand how their mind works tells them that you care. This encourages them to lean into the empathy that you're demonstrating. Your child will get the sense that, finally, someone understands them. Someone sees them for who they are and actually hears them. This feeling is vital to developing a healthy psyche, which will help them thrive as adults.

So, now that you understand what play therapy is all about and how beneficial it can be to you and your child, the next chapter will show how art and nature can help your child unleash the creativity that lies within.

Chapter 2: Art and Nature: Unleashing Creativity

This chapter will explore how you can work with nature and art to help your toddler be creative and expressive. Understanding nature and art is essential before diving into various activities meant to help your toddler flourish. You'll also understand why these activities have been chosen, and you'll be able to adapt them as needed to make them more effective for your child. Keep in mind that every child is different. Your child will have certain likes and dislikes that you must consider and adapt to as needed.

Why Art and Nature Matter

When it comes to play therapy, art and nature are necessary. First of all, art allows your child to express themselves fully. Children do not fully grasp verbal language and may, therefore, be limited in how they express themselves. So, using art, you can skip the difficulty of asking your child to express how they feel and instead let them express themselves using sculpting, painting, and other art forms. Art allows them to visually express their internal experiences, thoughts, and emotions. It's a great way for them to navigate the more complicated feelings that even adults still struggle to process. It's also a gateway to the unconscious aspects of their psyche and will allow you to understand what goes on in their head and what they need at any given time.

Art also matters because children get to work with metaphors and symbols to show you what they're going through. By looking closely at the meanings of these symbols, you, the therapist, and your child can all work together to figure out their emotional and psychological state of being.

Art can allow you to figure out your toddler's emotional state.

Nature is as essential as art because of the many sensory experiences that your child can enjoy. Your child will naturally feel calm and relaxed by interacting with flowers, trees, water, and other natural elements. This state of being is essential for them to express their feelings or get in touch with them. The beautiful thing about nature is its rich and multi-layered environment with all sorts of smells, sounds, colors, and textures that will engage your child's senses on every level. By getting your toddler outdoors, you allow them to connect with the world around them and feel a sense of being part of something bigger than they are.

Nature can also provide metaphorical language that you can use to understand where your child currently is on their emotional journey. For instance, the changing of the seasons could serve as a mirror for how your child feels. Winter may be an excellent way to express the concepts of loss or sadness, while spring can represent hope or feeling energized. By speaking with your child about nature and how it presents itself, your child may use what they learn about nature to express their feelings and better understand their emotional challenges. The next section of this chapter will discuss various activities you and your toddler can engage in. Some of these will be art-based, while others will be nature-based.

Art Activities

Finger Painting: Finger painting is a lovely art activity for your toddlers because they get to enjoy expressing themselves creatively as much as they want. On top of that, they'll enjoy various sensory experiences by working with the paint. Here are some of the materials you'll need for a fun finger painting session:

- Non-toxic paint of different colors
- Large, thick sheets of paper

- A disposable table cover. Alternatively, you can use newspapers to keep your work surface clean.

- Old clothes or a smock for your child to wear

- A damp towel or wet wipes to clean up after

Steps

1. Pick a good location for this activity. You can either set up an area of your living room for art or use a dedicated playroom. Your toddler should be able to move freely with no limitations.

2. You have to take care of the work surface. The last thing you want is paint stains. So, set down your disposable table cover or newspapers to keep the work surface clean.

3. Set up your work materials. The finger paint should be in containers that your toddler can reach easily. You can also use squeeze bottles instead. Set up the large sheets of paper on your work surface. You must ensure your toddler has all the room needed to make hand prints or whatever else they want to make.

4. Now, it's time to introduce your toddler to the activity. Sit them down and explain that you're both going to finger paint. Engage them by showing how stoked you are about the activity you're about to do together. You should also speak to them about it in a way they can understand. The goal is to show them you're excited so they can mirror your excitement and get into the activity with gusto.

5. Begin by demonstrating what your child should do. Place a finger into one of the colors and then stain the paper with it. If you prefer, you could plunge your whole hand into the paint because that would look more exciting to your child and encourage them to try it.

6. Now, let your toddler begin painting. Let them dip their fingers freely into the various colors to make swirls, prints, and any other shape they like. Resist the urge to give specific instructions or to demand that they do things a certain way.

7. As you paint with your toddler, get them to explore what it's like to touch the paint. Get them to notice how it feels on their hands, its texture, and its temperature. By doing this, you contribute directly to their sensory development.

8. As you work with your child, you should positively reinforce their efforts by praising them. Praise them for the colors they pick, the unique shapes they make, and how enthusiastic they are about the whole process. The more you encourage them, the more confident and expressive they will be.

9. Be open to allowing them to experiment. Suppose your toddler decides to dip a foot in the paint and use that instead of their hands. Don't stop them. Allow them to explore their imagination freely.

10. Remain in an open-ended conversation with your toddler as they paint. You should ask them open-ended questions. For instance, you can ask them what the paint feels like, what they like about their art, how they feel about what they're creating, and so on. The point here is to have a conversation encouraging them to express themselves and reflect on their actions and feelings.

11. When the fun and games are over, it's time for you and your toddler to clean yourselves up and put things away. Help your toddler clean their hands with a damp towel or wet wipes. It's also a good idea to display their art in the end. Don't forget to tell them how proud you are of their

work.

Playdough Sculpting: This is an excellent activity for your toddler because not only will they get to explore their creativity, but they will also enjoy various sensations as they work with their hands. Here's what you need:

- Non-toxic playdough in different colors. You can use a homemade version or buy some from the store.
- A work surface like a tray or a table
- Child-safe sculpting tools like rolling pins, cookie cutters, and so on

Steps:

1. Pick a good location that has adequate lighting and is comfortable.
2. Make sure the workspace is clean and safe. You may want to use a plastic tablecloth for easy clean-up.
3. Set up the various colors of playdough for your toddler. If you don't want to buy some from the store, you can create your own using flour, salt, water, and food coloring. Ensure you've got enough so your toddler can feel free to sculpt whatever they please.
4. Explain the activity to them using language they understand to get them pumped about the activity and sustain their interest and attention.
5. Begin by showing your toddler a few basic techniques for working with the playdough. For instance, you may roll it into a ball or create simple objects like snakes or triangles. Make sure that these demonstrations are simple enough for them to replicate.
6. As you work with your toddler, get them to talk about how they feel about the process. Get them immersed in the sensory experiences they have working with the playdough. Also, continue to encourage them for everything they create. Asking open-ended questions about what they're making or how they feel about what they're making is a good idea.
7. Playdough sculpting is an excellent way to boost your toddler's fine motor skills. So, show them how they can use their fingers to poke and pinch the dough. Show them how to shape things using rolling pins, cookie cutters, and other plastic utensils to give their sculpture more detail.
8. When you're done, congratulate them on doing a good job, and help them clean up with a damp towel or wet wipes. Remember to store your playdough in airtight containers or Ziploc bags for next time.

Collage Making:

These are the materials you need:

- Tissue paper, yarn, fabric scraps, feathers, magazines, colored paper, glitter, and other collage-friendly materials
- Child-safe scissors (these should only be used if your toddler is ready for them)
- Child-friendly glue or a glue stick
- A large cardboard or a large piece of paper

Steps

1. Once your space is all set up, explain to your toddler what you'll be doing together. Show them all the materials and explain all the different textures and colors. Get them to talk about how they feel about the textures they'll be working with to engage them. Remember to use child-friendly language and hype them up about what you're going to do.

2. Let them know that they have different options and don't have to stick to any one thing. Let them choose the materials they want.

3. Now, it's time to show them how to work with the child-friendly glue by demonstrating it. Make sure that you explain this process as you do it and that your language is clear and easy to understand.

4. Allow your toddler to enjoy exploring all of the materials. Let them touch and experiment with them however they want. They could tear them, cut them into different shapes, or work with them as they are.

5. As they work, encourage them to explore the sensations, congratulate them on what they're doing, and help them reflect and express themselves using open-ended conversations. When they're done, you should ask them why they chose certain things, what they love about their work, and so on.

6. When it's clean-up time, help your toddler tidy up themselves and put up their collage somewhere prominent to remind them of their accomplishment and to demonstrate to them that you are proud of them.

Sensory Bin Exploration: Sensory bin exploration is a great way to engage your child's senses. It's also good for emotional regulation. Here's how to go about it:

1. Prepare a sensory bin. In this bin, place all the things you know will give your toddler a sensory treat, like dry beans or water beads. Whatever material you choose to put in the bin must be safe for your toddler.

2. You can add other things to your sensory bin, such as little toys or objects from nature, like unique stones. Add objects that your child would be interested in.

3. Introduce your child to the activity, and explain to them that they will use their hands to feel everything in the bin. Tell them they should keep everything in the bin and be gentle as they play with the objects.

4. As your toddler feels around the bin, encourage them to notice the differences in textures, pour things through their hands and fingers, scoop things, and dig to discover the hidden items. Let them talk about what they feel and see, and teach them how to use words to express their different emotions and sensations. This is how you help them with language development. You should also be engaged in the play and show them you're enthusiastic and curious about the materials in the bin, too. You can do this by asking open-ended questions as you interact with them, making them feel supported and eager to play with the materials.

5. Encourage them to use their imagination as they play by creating various stories about the objects they find in the bin.

6. When you're done, encourage them to reflect by asking them questions – and pay attention to how they react. Take notice of what words they use as they speak with you, and pay attention to whatever else they're communicating with their body language and facial expressions while

exploring the bin.

7. Now it's time for you to clean up the materials and put them back in the bin if they spilled out.

Scribble Drawing: Scribble drawing can help your toddler refine their fine motor skills while encouraging them to express themselves. Here's how it works.

1. Get all the materials required, such as crayons, markers, and paper. Make sure you have a variety of colors for your toddler to choose from and that the materials are safe for their age.

2. Choose a good spot that has adequate lighting.

3. Explain to your toddler what you're going to do, and do your best to use language that they find exciting.

4. Start off by showing them what to do. Just scribble something on the paper with markers or crayons, demonstrating how they can create various shapes just by moving their hands and wrists.

5. Hand your toddler the marker and let them do things on their own. Let them understand what autonomy feels like by encouraging them to choose the colors they want to use and applauding their choices. Resist the urge to control them or give your input.

6. While your toddler scribbles, observe them and ask open-ended questions so they can express their feelings.

7. Ensure you continue praising your tot for their efforts and creativity. When you're done, take time to appreciate what they've done. You can even go a step further and ask them to tell you more about what they created.

8. When you're sure your toddler is done doodling or it's time for a different activity, put away the materials.

Nature Activities

I-Spy

1. You and your toddler need to be out in nature for this activity.

2. Begin by explaining how the game works. You need to describe the things that you see and have your toddler spot them.

3. You start by saying, "I spy something red," or "I spy a tall blade of grass." When you say this, your toddler should look for whatever it is you "spy" and point it out.

4. Now, it's your toddler's turn to spy something.

The benefit of this is that it sharpens their observational skills, improves their language skills, and gets them to connect with nature.

Nature Scavenger Hunt

1. For this, create a list of things you can find in nature. For instance, you could add a pine cone, a soft leaf, or a rough rock to your list.

2. Show this list to your child, and head out together to look for the items and collect them.

This activity encourages your child to explore more and sharpens their senses.

FIVE SENSES NATURE SCAVENGER HUNT

Tick each item off your list as you find it.

SIGHT

- [ ] Find something white
- [ ] Find something patterned
- [ ] Find something tiny
- [ ] Find something heart shaped
- [ ] Find something long
- [ ] Find five of the some thing

SOUND

- [ ] Find something that snaps
- [ ] Find an animal sound
- [ ] Find a soft sound
- [ ] Find something that crunches
- [ ] Find something loud
- [ ] Find something to make music with

TOUCH

- [ ] Find something bumpy
- [ ] Find something wet
- [ ] Find something warm
- [ ] Find something soft
- [ ] Find something prickly
- [ ] Find something smooth

SMELL

- [ ] Find a flower with a scent
- [ ] Find a smell you like

TASTE

- [ ] Find something humans could eat
- [ ] Find something an animal would eat

Playing with Mud

1. To avoid making a mess, do this outside the house. Set up an area with mud, some safe containers, and other utensils.
2. Your job here is to encourage your child to play with their imagination. You could encourage them by showing them how to make mud pies or an imaginary meal.
3. Make sure they don't get carried away and actually eat them.

Doing this will improve your child's creativity, imagination, and fine motor skills.

Collages

1. Gather natural materials such as twigs, flowers, leaves, branches, stones, etc.
2. Get some paper and glue for you and your toddler to use to create the collage.
3. Model the behavior you want them to copy by showing them how to tick the materials on the paper.
4. Let them arrange and stick the materials however they want.

Making collages with your child is an excellent way to boost their creativity and get them to explore their senses. They'll also feel a sense of accomplishment after having created their masterpiece.

Playing with Petals

1. For this, you need to get different colored flowers and bowls or containers.
2. Next, you and your toddler must sort the petals into different colors, placing them into different containers or bowls.

By doing this, you will help your child get better at recognizing colors and improve their sorting skills. You'll contribute to the development of their fine motor skills, and not only that, but you'll also encourage them to engage more with nature.

Playing with Sensory Bottles

1. Get some clear plastic bottles and fill them with leaves, pebbles, or sand.
2. When the bottles are filled, seal them as tightly as you can. You don't want your toddler opening them up.
3. Hand them the bottles and allow them to roll, shake, and have fun with them.

This will let them explore the various sounds and textures of each bottle.

Nature Painting

1. Use natural materials like twigs, pine cones, and leaves as brushes. You'll also need paper or a canvas to paint on.
2. Dip them yourself in some paint and hand them to your toddler. Let them dip their natural brush in the paint like you did.
3. Paint something on the paper, and encourage them to copy you or paint whatever they want.

This is different from regular painting in the sense that your toddler will be inspired by nature itself. As a direct result of engaging in nature painting, you'll notice your little one will get better at using their fine motor skills. You'll also fan the flames of curiosity in their little heart as they become a little researcher and experimenter who loves to tell you about what they've learned or noticed.

Rock Painting

1. Head out into nature with your toddler. Make it somewhere with loads of interesting rocks.
2. You can either collect as many smooth rocks as possible or have them do it.
3. Gather them all up in a pile.
4. Get some paint and markers, and let them go wild coloring the rocks.

Nature Storytelling

1. You and your toddler need to find a nice, comfortable position outside.
2. If other people are involved, get everyone to sit on the floor in a circle.
3. Next, encourage your toddler to pay attention to their environment while you tell them a story using the various objects around you in nature.

As you do this, you encourage your child to use their imagination. You also show them how to observe and improve their language skills.

Taking a Texture Walk:

1. For this, you and your toddler must take a walk in nature.
2. As you walk, encourage them to touch various natural surfaces like rocks, flowers, grass, tree trunks, etc.
3. As your toddler touches these surfaces, encourage them to share how they feel about them.
4. Let them talk about the ways the textures vary from one another.

The activity is great for improving a toddler's tactile awareness and helping them develop the necessary language to explain textures. In turn, this will get them to express difficult feelings and emotions.

Remember that for all these exercises to work, you need to always encourage your toddler to open up by asking them open-ended questions about how they feel. You can always relate different aspects of your chosen activity to their emotions. For instance, you could have your toddler hold on to a relatively rough rock and ask them what they think it would feel like to be a rough rock.

Chapter 3: Recognizing Toddler Behaviors

This chapter will explore the various factors responsible for why your toddler acts the way they do. To do this, you must first understand various theories of child development. There are a number of them, including attachment, cognitive, behavioral, and stage theories. However, some are more popular and better studied than others. As a parent, you need to have a rich understanding of these developmental theories so you're never at a loss for what's going on with your child. Everyone evolves with time, and they are no exception to the rule. These theories highlight what to expect from your child regarding how they feel and think and how they interact with the world.

Studying the way humans develop is a deep and layered topic. Everyone develops, but it's not easy to discover *what drives that development.* What makes your child act the way they do, and might that have something to do with how old they are? Does it involve the early relationships to which they have been exposed? Some psychologists say that children are born with unique temperaments, so you may wonder, could your child have a predisposition to behave in specific ways regardless of their social and environmental contexts? Developmental psychologists work hard to determine the answers to these perplexing questions to better understand a child's mind and explain or even possibly predict how your little one will likely act in their entire lifetime. This is the main focus of child development theories.

Freud's Psychosexual Developmental Theory

Freud had a rather interesting take on the development of a child. He did a lot of work with patients who were struggling with mental health, and in the process, he realized that how people act depends on the unconscious desires they carry and the experiences they had as a child. Freud believed that all sorts of conflicts happen in the various stages of life, which will inevitably affect your behavior and how you express yourself.

The psychosexual theory emphasizes that a toddler's development is expected to play out in stages. The developmental stages are rooted in whatever part of the body brings them the most pleasure and are expected to come with challenges that help children develop fully. Freud believed that the libido or sexual drive moves through various erogenous zones as the child moves from one stage of development to the next. If they do not successfully pass through a stage, this could result in them becoming fixated on the particular stalled point of their development. He believed that this is the reason adults act the way they do. In a situation where your child completes every stage of the developmental process successfully, odds are they will grow up to be a well-rounded individual.

Freud believed that when these conflicts aren't properly handled at each stage, the odds of the child successfully navigating what it means to be a grown-up would be slim to none. Fortunately, other development theories indicate that your child is not doomed and can actually change. As far as Sigmund Freud was concerned, there's no chance your child will be the same at age 50 as they would be at age 5, as there's no way they could continue to evolve.

Behavioral Child Development Theories

Behaviorism is a school of thought that rose to prominence in the first portion of the 20th century and would eventually become a prominent force in the field of psychology. According to behaviorists, psychologists must only pay attention to what they can observe before claiming to be true scientists. Regarding the behavioral perspective of child development, it is believed that all humans are the way they are as a result of their environment. Some of the more popular behaviorists were B. F. Skinner and John B. Watson. They believed that the only way to learn was by using reinforcement and association.

All behavioral theories operate on the premise that interactions with the environment are responsible for how a child acts, and these theories are only about what can be observed. There is no postulating or guessing what could be going on in the child's inner world. In other words, the child develops only as a response to punishment and reward. This theory holds that a child is shaped only through the stimuli they are exposed to and the language of reinforcement.

As you go through the other theories, you'll discover that this one is quite different because it does not hold any regard for emotions, thoughts, or feelings. Instead, it's just about the way the environment affects your child and vice versa. Looking at development through this lens, classical conditioning, and operant conditioning are the only ways through which your toddler can learn. With classical conditioning, they discover how natural occurrences are connected to prior events that they would otherwise consider neutral. With operant conditioning, they learn to adjust their behavior through the tools of reinforcement, repetition, and the risk of getting punished.

Erikson's Psychosocial Developmental Theory

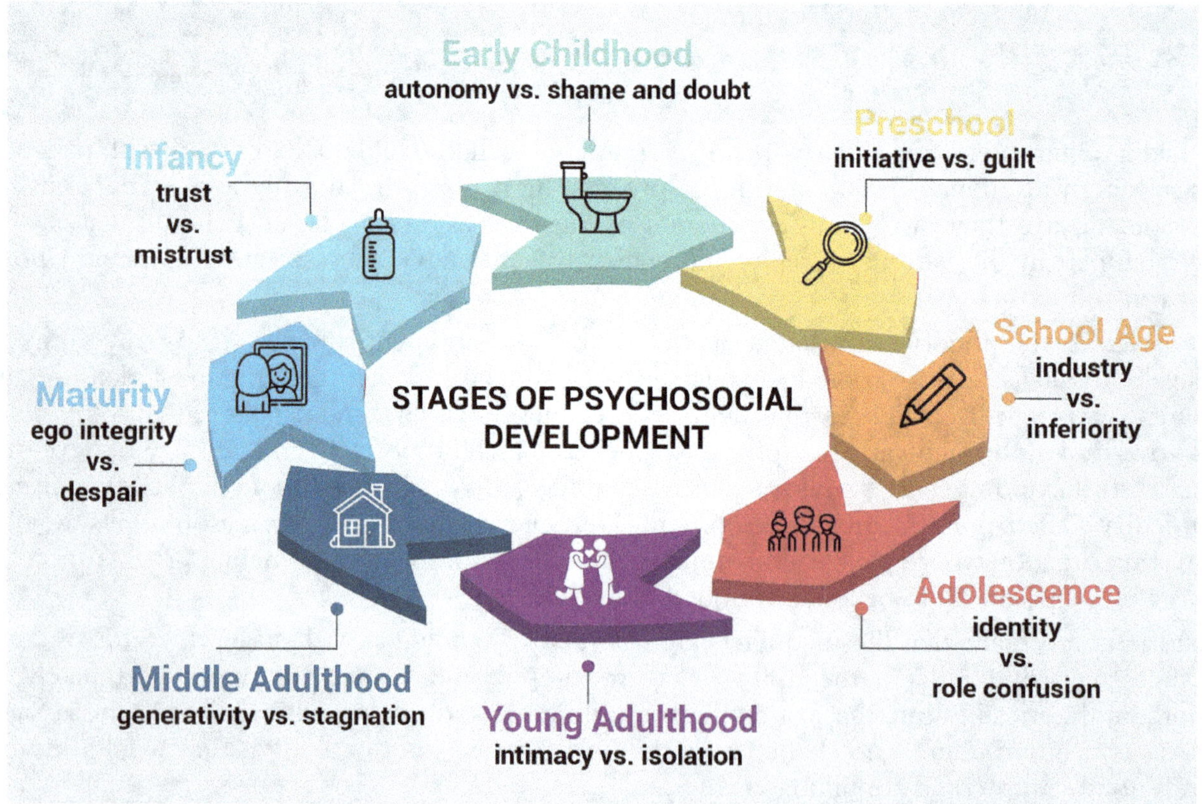

Not every psychologist necessarily agreed with Freud's take on development. Some would go on to develop their own ideas, and among them was Erik Erikson. In his theory of psychosocial development, there are eight distinct stages that properly encapsulate how people grow and change throughout their lives. These stages focus on social interaction and the various conflicts that come up at all these stages of development.

As far as Erikson was concerned, the only thing that matters is how your toddler views life and their various meaningful interactions as they go about meeting people and connecting with them. He didn't just assume the only years that matter are from ages 0 to 5, choosing instead to track toddler development from the womb to the tomb, so to speak. He also acknowledges that the unique conflicts attendant with each stage of development are crucial, as they'll affect your toddler's disposition later in life.

Bowlby's Attachment Theory

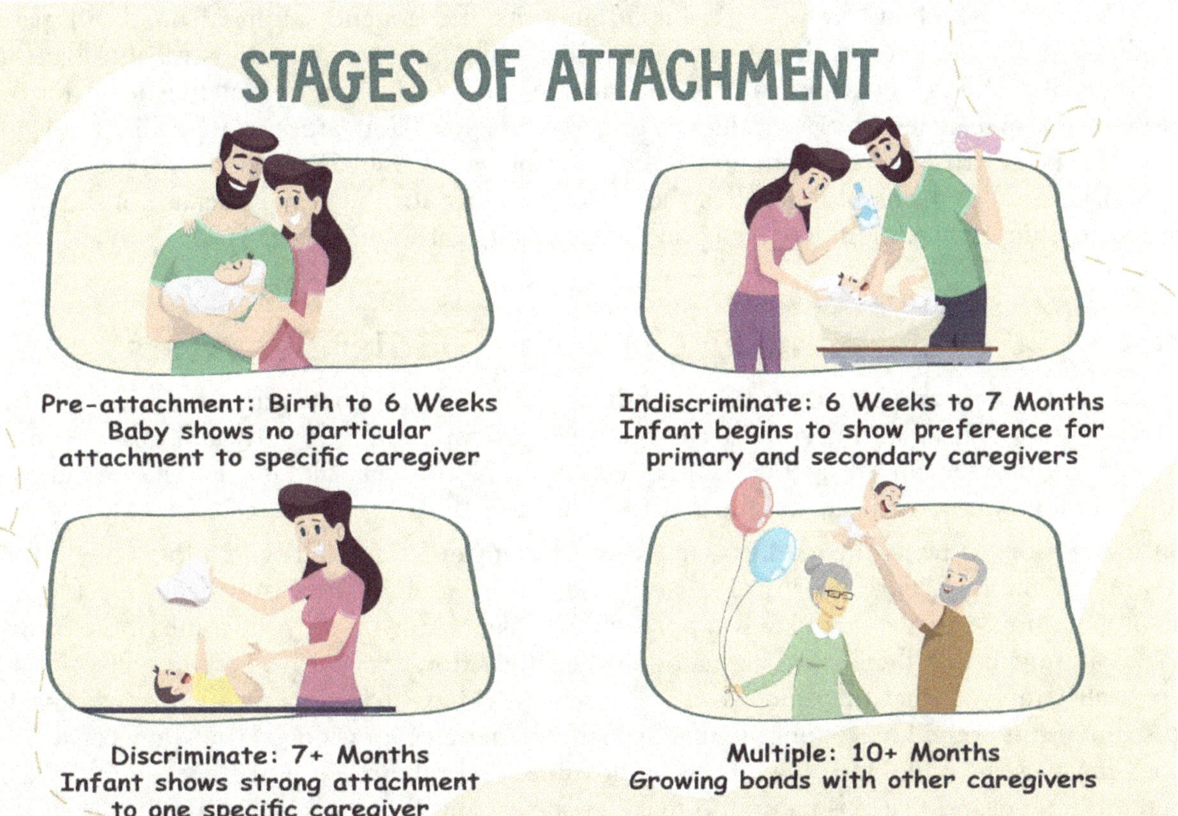

John Bowlby was more concerned with the social development of the child. He had one of the earliest theories on how this works, and he believed that the early relationships a child experiences are critical in the way that they develop throughout their life. His attachment theory indicated that children have a deep desire to be attached to others. These bonds are deep and powerful.

Think of them as invisible strings connecting you to your child, assuring them they're protected, loved, and always safe with you. You're both engaged in a dance orchestrated by nature itself, where you ensure you're always within arm's reach. Your child wants nothing more than to stick to you like glue, seeing you as their champion and hero who keeps them safe and lets them explore life around them.

Bowlby could tell that when this connection is honored by both the child and the caregiver, the little one enjoys a secure attachment style that does wonders for them in later years. However, with children who haven't been fortunate enough to have caregivers who are always present and ready to support them, their attachment style is anxious, avoidant, or ambivalent. These things will go on to affect the toddler's life as an adult profoundly, *and not in good ways.*

These are just a few of the numerous theories of child development available. As a parent or caregiver, it would be useful to learn more about these theories so you can begin to understand where your child is developmentally and what you need to do to help them make progress.

The Role of Genetics in Child Development

Child development is a dance between the environment and the child's genes. Some suggest that it is only the genes that affect the way a child develops. However, it is obvious that nature and nurture are both relevant to how the child evolves. The child inherits the genetic coding from both parents with instructions on how to express themselves physically, while the environment is responsible for shaping and crafting the child's behavior. The genes can also affect whether or not they'll be introverted or extroverted. Despite genes' obvious influence on physical expression, among other things, it is impossible to deny the power that the environment holds over how the child is molded. So, the point is to not relegate your child to the assumption that they cannot change for the better because of their genes. This is erroneous. The environment in which you find yourself is absolutely vital to who you are and who you become.

Understanding Common Toddler Behaviors

Your toddler is slowly growing towards having their own opinions. They may not understand the various emotions and thoughts that one could have, but if you took the time to study and observe your toddler, you would begin to decipher why they act the way they do. With that said, it's time to look at some of the meanings of their body language and the tantrums that they throw.

Gaze Aversion: When your toddler actively avoids your eyes, that tells you a lot. They'd like a break from your attention. Believe it or not, just because they're a child does not mean that they want your constant attention. As they gradually approach the age of two, they become more conscious of themselves enough that they can feel shame. When they don't want to meet your eyes, that tells you they're well aware of what they did wrong. When you notice that your toddler is averting their gaze because they did something wrong, you should help them acknowledge what they've done with the simplest language possible. Do so as gently as possible. Help them see how they can fix their mistakes. Help them understand that it is natural to make mistakes, and that does not mean they're a bad person. Get them to understand that they can always redeem themselves by correcting the damage they may have caused or expressing remorse for their actions.

Needing to Sleep with Stuffed Animals: When it's nighttime, your toddler wants to feel as safe and secure as possible. So, you may notice that they have a whole bunch of stuffed animals around them to feel protected. You see, your child has an active imagination that is great at envisioning monsters beneath the bed or in the dark corners of their room. This active imagination can also fuel their nightmares. Therefore, to feel at ease enough to fall asleep, your toddler will surround themselves with familiar and comforting objects, believing that they will be a form of protection against the monsters they perceive in the dark.

So, the proper thing to do is validate your toddler's need for safety and comfort and remind yourself that just because the monsters are imaginary, it does not mean they are any less real or scary to your toddler. Allow them to choose the comforting things they'd like to take to bed. Toddlers enjoy the process of making decisions, so you can ask them which books, toys, and animals they'd like to take with them. If you're concerned that they're taking too much with them, you can put a cap on how many they can take.

Hiding Their Face in Their Shirt Around Unfamiliar People: Believe it or not, just like adults, toddlers can struggle with social anxiety. You'll notice this by the various hiding behaviors that they demonstrate. This is because they don't understand how to navigate the process of socializing and dialogue just yet. They would rather console themselves using various physical and sensory expressions. You'll notice they keep tugging at their clothes to distract themselves and will even chew on them. Sometimes, they'll grasp you tightly with that infamous grip strength that toddlers inexplicably possess – likely because you represent their anchor when they are floundering in the deep blue sea of socialization. To soothe their nervous little heart, they may suck on their thumb like it's the most delicious candy they've ever had. When they're feeling really shy and nervous, they'll cover their faces using their shirts because the way they see it, if they can't see you, you can't see them, and that thought brings them immense comfort.

The way to handle social anxiety is to be gentle about it. Encourage your little one to break out of their fortress. Usually, they always look to you to figure out how they should react when they find themselves in an unfamiliar situation. So, think about what your body is telling them. If you're a bit tense, consider taking a deep breath and then exhaling to relax your shoulders, putting a smile on your face, and actively engaging with new people. Your child will model this behavior. It also helps if you use nonverbal language, such as giving your child a nice reassuring rub on their back or a squeeze on their shoulders to ensure they understand they're safe. Do not expect your child to immediately warm up to anyone they meet. Your part in all this is just to be patient with them and wait for them to warm up.

Hiding When They Poop: This tells you that your toddler would like some space and time for themselves to do their business. They do this because they have observed the adults around them doing the same thing. This is good because it tells you they're ready to be potty trained. You'll also realize that, at this point, they are very vocal about having their diaper changed. Usually, toddlers become ready to use the bathroom when they hit ages two and three. Respect their desire for privacy, but don't attempt to force them to use the bathroom just yet. All you have to do when you start to notice this behavior is guide them to the bathroom.

They Throw a Tantrum: When your toddler is acting out and throwing tantrums, they're trying to tell you they don't feel like themselves. Usually, this is not easy to deal with because it's often a shock to see your baby acting like something out of a horror movie. However, you don't have to be afraid. Just because your 2-year-old throws a tantrum does not mean this is who they are. It's simply their way of communicating with you to let you know that they need attention, are tired, or are simply bored. You have to attune yourself to what your toddler feels.

Toddlers usually throw tantrums because they don't feel like themselves.
https://www.pexels.com/photo/desperate-screaming-young-boy-6624327/

When dealing with tantrums, most parents attempt to reason with their toddlers, but this is not the time for that. Often, attempting to be rational with your toddler is useless. Instead, you must figure out what is the actual cause of their tantrum and let them know that you are aware of how they're feeling, even if you don't fully understand. You must do all you can to validate their emotions because this is what will lead them to calm down gradually.

The Tantrum Continues Even After They Get What They Want: If you're dealing with a situation where they continue to act out even after they have got what they wanted, you must remember that you're dealing with someone who's naturally impatient. They're still a baby. They don't quite understand what it means to delay gratification just yet. At this age, your toddler wants instant fulfillment. You need to be firm and not immediately give in to their needs. Instead, let them know that you have heard them out and will give them what they want in due time. This is an excellent opportunity to teach them to be patient, and with time, you can increase how long it takes between them expressing their desires and you fulfilling said desires. That is how you teach them to be patient.

Being Possessive When Other Children Are Around: Sometimes, your toddler exhibits clingy, possessive behavior, and it's difficult to understand why. This tells you that they think they don't have your attention or not enough of it. You can bank on this being the case if you've been a little too busy recently or if there's a new baby in your home. When there haven't been any changes in how you've been spending time with them, or there's no new baby, odds are that this possessiveness simply indicates that they are becoming increasingly aware of themselves. It's a phase where children become obsessively possessive of their parents, but you must understand that's not bad. It tells you that they are starting to become aware of their personhood. At this point, they identify themselves as being connected to the things that have the most value to them, and as their caregiver, you are at the top of that list.

So, how do you handle a possessive child? You should give them a hug. Let them know that, yes, you definitely are their parent or caregiver. Express to them in no uncertain terms how much you love them. You can also take advantage of this by teaching them about the importance of sharing. You can tell them that you are their parent, true, but it is okay to be kind to other people.

Activities to Understand Your Little One Better

Shower your toddler with affection and encouragement. When you show your child affection, you demonstrate tenderness and love to them. You show them warmth in your interactions with them. How do you do this? First, you begin with physical touch. Touch is the primary language children use to begin understanding the world around them. So, little things like kisses, hugs, holding hands, cuddling, or rubbing their backs could comfort them. When you do these things, they feel like you love them, and they feel safe and secure.

Eye contact is another excellent way to demonstrate affection to your toddler. As you speak or play with them, always look in their eyes warmly. Eye contact is a nonverbal way to let them know that you have your full attention, whatever they're talking to you about matters.

Affection also implies quality time every day. You could read a book with them, talk about their day, or play with toys. The important thing is to be present. Some parents assume that spending time with their children means being in the same room while doing their thing, but that's not right. Turn off the television and put your phone down. Your child should have your full attention as you actively engage them.

Also, listen attentively and actively to your toddler. Do what you can to understand them, respond to them, and remember what they tell you. It doesn't matter how trivial what they're saying appears to be. Remember that it means the world to them in their little heart.

As for encouragement, don't just praise your toddler when they get something right. Praise them for also putting in the work. Praise them for their effort. If they tried to draw a chair, and it didn't turn out like a chair, you can commend them for trying and being creative rather than reprimand them for making mistakes.

Encouragement means celebrating the small wins, like when they finally learn how to tie their shoelaces or decide to share with a playmate. As you encourage your child, you create an environment where they can safely express themselves. You allow them to do things for themselves instead of taking away a learning moment by doing it for them. You act as a support and assist as a guide to them while you allow them to take charge. By offering support, you encourage them to feel confident and independent. Also, never compare your child to another because that would damage their self-worth and inhibit their abilities and personal growth.

Make a habit of reading to your child every day. Reading with your child is more than a bedtime routine. It's an opportunity for them to learn, develop emotionally, and connect with you on a deeper level. Consistency matters, so set aside a specific time for your child to read with you daily. Having a specific part of the house dedicated to reading is helpful. Make it nice and comfortable so you're child always wants to be there when it's time.

Don't keep reading the same book to them. Instead, have a diverse selection. The books should vary in topics and styles and suit your child's age. You can make reading fun by taking your child to the library and letting them pick the books that they're most interested in. As you encourage them to read, you help them develop cognitively, and their language skills improve. Since most stories have moral lessons, your child can learn about ethics and values, which will help build their character. You also foster a spirit of curiosity within your child.

Show your little ones how to express themselves in healthy ways when they're upset. Emotions are unavoidable. They're part of being human. Your child will begin demonstrating emotions at a young age. So, giving them the tools they need to manage and express how they feel healthily is a great idea. This skill isn't something people are born with. It's an ability that is learned.

So, how do you teach your child how to express themselves? First, you must model healthy expression. Your child watches you keenly and will act the way you do. When you're upset, speak clearly about your feelings calmly, breathe deeply, and resist the urge to be hostile.

Encourage your child to talk about their feelings by talking about yours. You can tell them, "I felt upset that time..." or, "I felt relieved when..." It's great when children see that everyone has different emotions and that it's okay to feel how they do. Validate your toddler's feelings by listening to them actively and not dismissing them. To comfort their children, some parents say things like, "It's not a big deal" or "Don't cry." Never discourage your child from crying if that's how they feel. Instead, you could say, "I can tell you're not feeling so great right now. How about we talk about it when you feel like you can?"

Another way to teach your child to handle their emotions healthily is to show them different coping mechanisms, such as breathing exercises. Show them how to count to 10 when everything feels too much. Teach them to use art to express themselves. Have them go outside and get active to release their emotions through running, jumping, shaking, or anything else. Role-play situations where you and your child act out different emotions and how to respond to them in various contexts. Rather than only comfort your child, teach them how to make empowering decisions to feel better at the moment.

Set boundaries that are appropriate for their age. Boundaries are essential because they help your child feel safe and secure and give them structure. They understand why certain behaviors are necessary and know what is expected of them and what to expect from them. Your child may not be able to carry a glass of water at their age safely. So, a reasonable boundary would be using a safe sippy cup until they accomplish the physical milestone where they can safely carry a glass of water.

If your child is younger, they may be unable to express their more complex emotions. So be patient with them and give them the tools that they can use to tell you how they feel. Those tools include the necessary vocabulary or charts displaying emotions in a fun way. Remember what your toddler is capable of in terms of cognition. You can't expect a 3-year-old to be okay with waiting for something for a long time. So, rather than criticize them for impatience, you can find ways to distract them.

Whenever you set a boundary with your child, give them choices. It doesn't help just to tell them no. If they would like to have some candy before dinner, you could give them the option of a healthy snack or choosing what they'll have for breakfast the next day.

Whenever your child respects and follows boundaries, positively reinforce compliance by appreciating them and offering them a reward. Also, explain the rationale behind the boundaries you set. Your child may not understand why it's not okay to hit or bite. By letting them know it's not okay because it hurts other people, they're more likely to respect those boundaries in the future.

As your child grows, you can allow the boundaries to morph with them so that you account for their increasing capabilities and offer them more freedom and responsibilities. You can let them decide when to go to bed or what to wear out. You can also work together when creating rules so they don't feel you're just giving them orders.

Model the social skills and emotional skills you'd like your toddler to have. Children copy the older ones in their lives who have more experience of being on earth than they do. Give them the correct blueprint to follow. Show them what it's like to be calm in the face of stress or intense feelings. Demonstrate how to actively listen, share and take turns, and behave politely. Show them the importance of owning up to mistakes and apologizing when it comes to conflict. Teach them how two people can devise a satisfying solution when faced with a disagreement.

Teach them empathy by acknowledging how they feel when distressed or pleased about something. Show them what it means to be kind. As you demonstrate these behaviors, narrate them to your child. Let them know why you do what you do, and they'll model that. Whenever you slip up (and you will, because you're human), show them what it's like to self-reflect. If you raise your voice at someone, you can say, "I was upset, but I shouldn't have raised my voice. That was wrong of me. Next time, I'll handle my emotions better and be kinder."

Chapter 4: Role-Playing — Perception and Empathy

This chapter will show various engaging role-playing activities to help your toddler understand and express their emotions.

The Importance of Role-Playing Games

Role-playing games are vital when it comes to developing empathy and being able to take on other perspectives. As you role-play, your child has a challenge set before them. They need to take on a different persona, which makes it possible for them to develop empathy as they understand other people's feelings and thoughts and can appreciate someone else's perspective.

With role-playing, you can teach your child to put themselves in someone else's shoes so they can see how the world works through new eyes. This is essential for developing empathy. Empathy is vital for socialization, and it's a skill that your child needs to learn if they're going to stand a chance of developing successful social connections and handling conflict effectively and productively.

Having your child role-play will encourage socialization.

You can use certain games to help your child get in touch with their emotions, practice socializing, and learn how to effectively pass across their point of view to other people while being respectful. So, when you encourage your child to take on a different persona or perspective, you offer them the opportunity to understand themselves even more and understand others.

Understanding Empathy

Empathy has two aspects to it: the emotional aspect and the cognitive aspect. Emotional empathy is being able to experience what someone else feels emotionally, while cognitive is being able to imagine what someone else is dealing with emotionally. For instance, if your child sees that their friend is in tears, emotional empathy will move your child to want to help this person out. However, suppose your child is only working with cognitive empathy. In that case, they only understand that the other child is dealing with sadness and needs to be comforted somehow. Cognitive empathy is something your child will get used to much later in life, as your child understands they have a much different perspective and experience than others.

Empathy matters because your child needs to learn why rules matter and what makes something right or wrong. Not only that, but they will also discover behaviors that are beneficial to socializing, such as assisting others. Empathy will help your child successfully navigate their social life, an intricate part of being human. On top of that, your child will enjoy quality relationships that last long as they master empathy.

Teaching Your Child Empathy

When you want to teach your child how to be empathetic, you must serve as a role model by being warm and caring. Odds are they will act the same way with other people. Also, you should teach them to understand their emotions better and label them appropriately. Remember, being empathetic relies heavily on the ability to experience someone else's feelings or imagine what they may be going through. Therefore, you cannot escape teaching your little one about emotions; this is how you can get them to become empathetic. Labeling emotions and explaining what emotions feel like will make it easier for them to understand how others feel and be concerned about those who aren't having a good time.

You must validate every emotion your child feels, even when it is uncomfortable. Unfortunately, certain parents would rather minimize their children's feelings. They never allow them to express themselves and choose to shut them down before they can even get a word in edgewise. Don't be this kind of parent. You must explain that how they feel always matters. Help them understand that just because someone else feels differently does not automatically mean their own feelings are invalid. Show them that you care about their feelings, and you're essentially modeling excellent, empathetic behavior for your child to copy.

You also have to be okay with letting your child know how you feel at any point in time and why you feel that way. Emotions can be tricky and complicated things for a child to understand. That is mainly why toddlers choose to throw a tantrum instead of communicating what's bothering them. When you take the time to express how and why you feel a certain way, you're modeling behavior that encourages your little one to turn within and do some introspection. You also make it easier for them to rely on their intuition because they understand that their feelings are not to be dismissed. They will learn that they must recognize the causes of their feelings. This will do wonders for your child later on when they're an adult interacting with others who may be manipulative or have ill intentions.

Role Playing Games

1. **Emotions Charade**: With this game, your child can play with you or with a group of other children. One person acts out emotions while the others are left to understand or try to guess what that person is portraying and feeling. This is an excellent way to engage your child and have them understand how emotions work. Here are some emotions to consider: happiness, sadness, boredom, anger, and excitement.

2. **Family Role Reversal**: With this exercise, your child can pretend to be other family members, such as a sibling or a parent. The idea is to work with their imagination. Your child is meant to take on the various responsibilities and tasks connected to the people they're portraying. By taking on different family roles, your child is better able to understand the responsibilities on everyone's shoulders and be empathetic towards them.

3. **Puppet Show:** In this game, you and your children should use puppets to try to express different real-life situations and the emotions attached to these situations. This will help your child learn how to communicate clearly and creatively. Real-life scenarios could include being in a position to help someone else, comforting someone who has lost a pet, dealing with a sore loser, and so on.

4. **Story Role Swap:** This game involves seeing the world through someone else's eyes. You and your child should take turns telling a story from various characters' perspectives. You could

work with any story you want and get creative with it. You can use real-life stories or work with fairy tales.

5. **Animal Adventures:** You and your child will take turns acting like different animals, thinking about how the animal might feel in various scenarios. This is great for helping your child learn empathy, even towards animals. It's also a good way to help your child learn respect for wildlife. They can learn what it means to feel as powerful and dangerous as a lion or as fragile as a bird.

6. **Helping Hands:** In this game, there are two roles: the helper and the one being helped. You and your child need to take turns acting in these roles. As you do this, your child will begin to understand the importance of reaching out to others to help, as well as asking for help when something gets to be a bit too much.

7. **What Am I Doing and Feeling?:** This game involves copying each other. Start off by performing facial expressions or movements and then letting your child copy you. Then, you can let your child take the lead. This activity results in your child becoming more attentive to people around them, and they learn how to deduce the implications of other people's actions and choices.

8. **Mirroring Emotions:** By playing this game, your child has to figure out what the faces you make mean emotionally. So, this implies that your child must understand the various emotions one could experience before they can successfully play. When your child gets it wrong, you can just help them understand by explaining.

9. **Drawing Faces:** With this exercise, your child should draw various faces that demonstrate different emotions. They don't even have to be good at drawing. They simply need to get the basic attributes of a face. As your child draws, you can engage them in conversation about what it is that could make someone feel whatever emotion they're depicting.

10. **Empathy Drama:** In this game, you and your child will take on different personas and even dress the part to reenact scenarios. As for characters that you may want to play, consider the various people who don't have an easy time of it at school or at work. So, think about the new child in school, the painfully shy one, the one who gets picked on, the one who is always alone, and so on. You can have your child play each of these roles and then have them play themselves while you take on the roles. As you play, you should ask them how they feel when they portray any of these characters, what they'd like to do to help them, or what they'd prefer others to do in that situation.

Tips for Supporting Your Child During Role Play

- Do your best to remain present and engaged as you carry out these activities.

- During each of the previous activities, don't forget to model empathy.

- Encourage your child to think about the things they learned from each activity.

- Always offer your child positive feedback for trying, and encourage them whenever they feel challenged.

- Make sure that the environment in which you role-play is safe so that your child feels comfortable expressing or trying things they've never done before.

Chapter 5: Applying Attachment Theory

People have always sought to understand the causes of development in terms of emotions. As a result, a certain theory that closely examines childhood's early days has been developed. This theory is known as the attachment theory. In the early days of childhood, the child's heart is fragile, and their soul is only just budding, becoming a fully-fledged human being. The attachment theory seeks to explain the process of the child's development emotionally.

Attachment theory sheds light on the emotional bond between the child and their caregiver. With this theory, you have a vivid picture of how human relationships work, as it captures emotions such as love, the idea of trust, and the importance of security, which all come together to form the child's sense of self. These elements will act as the blueprint for how your child will interact with everyone else as they mature.

Children tend to be attached to their caregivers.

When it comes to play therapy, the attachment theory shows how to help your child develop healthily regarding their emotions. When your child has the space to play, it opens up their heart so they can show you what they truly are afraid of, what they're curious about, and what it is they desire from life. By working with play, your child can set off on a journey of discovering who they really are, and attachment theory acts as their North Star, showing them the way to their authentic self.

The Basics of Attachment Theory

This theory, developed by John Bowlby, posits that all the relationships and interactions you and your little one share will profoundly impact how the child develops emotionally, socially, and cognitively all through their life. According to this theory, your child desires to be as close and connected to you, the primary caregiver, as much as possible. You act as a base of security from which your child can head out to explore the world and return to you when they need to be comforted or reassured that everything is fine.

Another aspect of attachment theory is attachment behaviors. Your child will show specific behaviors meant to help them remain as close to you as possible so they can continue to enjoy your care and love. Among these behaviors are smiling, reaching out for you, cooing adorably, or crying. These behaviors are essential because they help the toddler survive. Not only that, but when they are responded to appropriately, they help your toddler develop a secure attachment to you.

There are also attachment styles to consider. According to this theory, your toddler will develop an attachment style that depends on their experiences with you. There are three main attachment styles to consider. The first one is the secure attachment, where your toddler feels securely attached to you in the sense that they are confident you will always be there for them. They know that if they reach out to you, you will respond. Because they know this, they feel safe heading out into the world, knowing that they can always come back to you if anything goes wrong.

The next style of attachment is known as the insecure avoidance attachment. When a toddler has this attachment style, they don't really care whether or not they are separated from the person who's supposed to care for them. They don't demonstrate much in the way of distress and will usually either avoid the caregiver or ignore them completely.

The final attachment style is the insecure, resistant, or anxious attachment style. Here, the toddler demonstrates very clingy behavior. If your child is this way, you'll notice that they're very anxious. Whenever they're not with you, they become very distressed. However, when you return, they're lukewarm to you at best as they both want to be comforted by you all while resisting it.

The Importance of a Secure Attachment Style

A secure attachment is essential because it will allow your toddler to become emotionally secure. This attachment style contributes to the development of your toddler's brain. Those who are securely attached tend to be more curious about life, more creative when it comes to solving problems, and generally perform better when it comes to cognitive functions.

Another thing to note about the security attachment style is that it is excellent for reducing the risk of various mental conditions like depression, anxiety, and other disorders in later life. When a child has an insecure attachment, it makes it difficult for them to navigate their emotions, and of course, interpersonal relationships become a source of pain. By choosing to understand the attachment theory, you can do all you can in your power to promote secure attachments between you and your child to give them the best shot at life, and there's no better way to accomplish this than through play therapy.

How to Foster Secure Attachment

Play therapy is necessary for creating a secure attachment between you and your toddler. For one, it creates an environment where your toddler can feel safe and trust you fully. In this situation, working with a therapist, you and your toddler can enjoy a space that is welcoming to each other and has clear boundaries so your child can feel safe and secure.

The excellent thing about play therapy and developing a secure attachment style is that it is a non-directive approach. Your child does not need to take orders, making it easy for them to take the lead. They get to be the ones to set the tone for every activity, while your therapist is only a facilitator, and you only serve as an observer. This way, you allow them to express themselves as fully and freely as they want without interrupting or judging them. There's much to learn from simply watching the way your child plays.

To foster secure attachments, you're working with play as a language. Your child may not be able to understand much else, depending on their age, but they do understand what it means to play. Thanks to play, they can express their emotions and thoughts, and they can share their inner experiences with you in ways that are easy for them. Children do not yet have the language necessary to paint their inner landscape in terms of emotions and thoughts. Play is a great way to encourage them to do this, which will, in turn, ensure a secure attachment between you and your toddler.

Part of fostering a secure attachment is allowing your child access to various therapeutic tools and materials that excite them. Among these are puppets and dolls, and there are art supplies and other objects that could be of symbolic importance to them. The idea is to offer as many things as possible that allow the child's imagination to feel free and roam wild. By doing this, you encourage your children to be themselves and feel that you are their safe space.

During play therapy activities, you and your therapist should actively listen to your child, paying attention to the various ways in which the child expresses themselves through play and the words they choose to share their thoughts. The therapist is engaged in reflective listening in the sense that they will reflect everything your child is sharing back to them to validate their emotions. This will lead to the development of empathy. You can mirror this behavior at home to encourage your child to feel securely attached to you.

Using play therapy, you can encourage secure attachment by teaching your child emotional coping skills as well as regulation skills. Using play, your child can learn how to figure out what they're feeling and then healthily express those feelings. They can learn how to identify when they're out of sorts and use various techniques to help them control themselves.

Play Therapy Activities to Foster Secure Attachment

1. **Puppet Time:** This activity involves you and your child playing with dolls or puppets. You should take turns playing different roles, such as the child or caregiver. This way, your child will understand empathy and communication, and you both understand each other, which is conducive to developing a secure attachment.

Playing with puppets can help your child form a secure attachment.

2. **Team Adventure Quest:** This activity is – essentially – anything you and your child can do together to develop your bond. This could include anything from physical activities to board games or puzzles. The idea is you want to be able to solve problems, make decisions, and collaborate with each other. Some examples of these games may include trying to solve a puzzle together, building an obstacle course or a fort and completing it together, and so on. Whatever you choose, ensure your child can handle it by considering their age and that you're both having a good time while you connect and cooperate with each other.

3. **Imagination Station:** For this game, you and your toddler pretend that you're on a train that needs to get somewhere and is powered by stories. You're going to start a story, and then you'll have your toddler continue, and then you pick it up from wherever they leave off. As you do this, you will be allowing them and yourself the opportunity to explore emotions, solve problems, and discuss the subject of relationships. All of these things will serve to increase the bond between you. When the story ends, you and your toddler can make-believe arriving at your final destination and getting off the train.

4. **Colorful Fun:** This activity is a simple one. You and your child get to pick whatever medium of art you want to use to express yourselves, as long as it involves loads of colors, and then get into it. You can discuss how you feel and express yourself as you work on your art. You can talk about various things that your child is experiencing at school, allowing them to open up to you. Working with art allows your child to connect with their emotional side, which means you understand their inner world even better and create a secure attachment to your child.

5. **Superhero Switch-Up Showdown:** You and your child can participate in this role-playing game. You should take turns being a superhero, using various superhero powers, and share the roles of caring for and saving others.

6. **Rhythm Safari Dance Party:** With this, you need to turn your living room into a dance floor. You can give it a fun theme, like animals, for instance. You and your child can dance, sing, and even play instruments while you pretend to be various animals. Encourage your child when they demonstrate creativity in their movement. By using dance, you and your child can develop a stronger bond. Also, there's the benefit of the laughter that you will definitely share in the process.

7. **Wilderness Explorers Expedition:** If your child is old enough, you can take them on a wilderness adventure. All you have to do is find a local park or some nearby nature reserve. You both go on a nature walk where you get to identify animals and plants, and at the end, you can make some art using twigs, leaves, and other natural bits and pieces that you have gathered. By creating a shared experience, you will improve your toddler's appreciation for nature and have the opportunity to communicate openly with each other to discover your emotional landscapes together. All this contributes to being securely attached to each other.

8. **Mystery Investigators Unite:** Tell your child that your home is now a detective's lair. If there are other members of the family, this is great because you can all come together and pretend to solve a mystery. To do this, you will have to create various clues, hide messages all over the place, and place puzzles throughout the house. This is an excellent game to encourage your toddler to communicate with you, collaborate with others, and figure out how to solve problems. It can not only improve the bond that you and your toddler share but also the bond between them and other members of the family.

9. **Magical Time Machine Journey:** This storytelling method will improve the bond between you and your child. You both need to take turns telling stories traversing through time and space. You and your child can create amazing scenes and sensations, relax with each other, and connect. Your story can cover anything from futuristic worlds to ancient civilizations. You could even decide to delve into the realm of magic.

10. **Cosmic Sensation Adventure:** Working with bags full of glitter, some water, and various shapes in confetti colors, you can create a sensory experience that your child will love. Both of you should explore the various sensations in this bag. You might also want to use some slime to make things even more fun. Encourage your child to squish the objects, move the bags around to form various lumps, and work with their imagination.

Practical Advice for Parents and Caregivers

- Take every opportunity to cultivate empathy by trying to see the world through your child's eyes and understand how they feel and see things.

- Be responsive to your child. Whatever their needs may be and whatever cues they give you, respond right away.

- Be consistent in your responsiveness. Responding to them one minute and ignoring them the next isn't a good idea; that's how you create trust issues and a feeling of uncertainty in your child that will plague them for the rest of their life.

- You must engage your toddler in therapy play every day. These games are about communicating with each other, sharing your experiences, and exploring the emotions you both feel.

- Always be clear in your instructions. You need to be clear about the rules of each game so that your child understands what to do and you have a better time together.

- Encourage your child to be open and to communicate with you by ensuring there's no room for them to wonder if it's safe to say what's on their mind without being put down or shut up.

- Encourage the spirit of teamwork. This will go a long way in helping your child learn to collaborate with others, solve problems, and make decisions as part of a team.

- Your little one is not too young to understand the concept of appreciation. Therefore, whenever your child's making an effort, you should celebrate that. Let them know that you see what they're doing and that they are doing great.

- Active listening is an essential skill that you can teach your child by modeling it. Not only should you pay attention to what they say, but you should also tell them that you understand by reflecting all those experiences and emotions back to them. That is how you validate their feelings to help them to be a well-rounded individual.

- Nothing should be so important that you don't get to spend quality time with your little one. You should dedicate time each day to spend with your child. That is how you encourage a secure bond with them.

Chapter 6: Sensory Strategies

This chapter will introduce various activities that will stimulate and engage your child's senses.

What Is Sensory Play?

Sensory play is the sort of play that involves stimulating the senses, including sight, touch, smell, taste, and hearing. Sensory play is necessary for your little one's brain to develop as it should. It is the basis for developing other skills, including social and cognitive capabilities.

Why Sensory Play Is Vital

Sensory play is a great way to help your child develop physically, cognitively, and emotionally. It engages your toddler's senses on various levels. Sensory experiences are a great way for them to be stimulated, providing their brain with the fuel it needs to be capable of more complex cognitive skills. By allowing your toddler to work with various colors, shapes, and textures, they'll be much better at processing information from their senses, developing better spatial awareness, and solving problems.

Sensory play engages your toddler's senses.
https://www.pexels.com/photo/girl-holding-yellow-plastic-cup-full-of-macaroni-3933271/

Another reason sensory play is vital for your toddler is that it helps them integrate information from their senses to understand their environment. In the future, they will be well aware of where they are, how to handle themselves, and how to stay safe. By working with various sensations, your toddler will be much better at processing sensory input and organizing that information. This will inevitably lead to a much better ability to focus for extended periods, hold their concentration on something, and regulate the way they respond to external stimuli.

Sensory play is great for your child's fine and gross motor skills and proprioceptive and vestibular systems. By engaging your toddler in sensory play, you'll notice they get better at manipulating small objects such as pens, pencils, or crayons, scooping, pouring, and squeezing materials from one container into another. All of these will inevitably do wonders for their motor coordination, and it will improve their dexterity, too. Your child's gross motor skills improve as they climb tables and trees, maintain their balance on a leg or a ledge (proprioceptive), jump from one spot to another (vestibular), etc. Not only that, your child's coordination and strength will improve.

Sensory play can also be a wonderful thing for the development of language. The more your child explores various sensory objects, the more they talk about them in conversations with you and describe their experience, then the more they'll learn how to work with words to communicate their ideas. They will understand the words related to sensations, textures, colors, and more. This is a great way to improve their lexicon and their ability to communicate.

Sensory play is great for the regulation of emotions. It offers a controlled and safe environment for your child to explore everything around them and express how they feel about it. The sensory stimuli you provide your child can stimulate their interests. It calms them down when they feel too anxious or irritable. This is a great way to teach your child how to regulate their emotions and soothe themselves when they're not feeling so great. You may offer your child a stress ball that they can squeeze whenever they're feeling tense, and you can also let them play with soft and soothing materials to allow them to feel relaxed whenever they're a little too stressed out.

Social interaction and communication are two things that are also improved by sensory play. As your child engages in these activities with other children and with you, they learn the importance of sharing and taking turns. They discover that sometimes you can cooperate with others and that when things are difficult, you can always negotiate. This will help them get better at socializing with others and being empathetic. Also, sensory play is excellent for your little one to understand other people's perspectives by choosing to collaborate with them.

Your child's imagination and creativity will soar as a result of engaging in constant sensory play. The materials you work with tend to be open-ended in nature, which means that there are so many possibilities for your child, and they can come up with so many different scenarios. They take what's just a regular pile of sand and shape it into a castle or a ball, or they could use playdough to create all kinds of things. This encourages them to think divergently and to get better at problem-solving.

Sensory play is great because every child is naturally curious about the world surrounding them. When you actively set up sensory play activities, your child gets to enjoy satisfying the desire to explore, experiment, and discover life. Through these experiences, your child will become even more wondrous about the world around them and will want to consume even more knowledge.

Different Types of Sensory Play

Various kinds of sensory play are classified according to the senses they engage. Each of them matters because they will help your child learn about the world around them and how to interact safely and enjoyably.

First, you have the sort of sensory play that requires working with the sense of touch. These activities include playing with water, sand, clay, or play dough. This will offer your child various opportunities to figure out the different textures, sensations, and temperatures.

There is also sight sensory play, which employs your child's sense of sight. This is exceptional for sharpening your child's sense of perception and cognitive skills. Among these are sorting activities, where your child arranges things according to shape or color, puzzles, or playing with shadow and light. All of these can help your child learn visual distinction and how to solve problems.

Sound sensory play will help your child's auditory perception and develop their linguistic skills. As they listen to some good music, create their own fun tunes, or play games that require listening to and making sounds, your child will become a fabulous listener, able to pick up subtle nuances that others miss in conversation. They will also develop a sense of rhythm.

Taste sensory play is a great way to help your child learn about their preferences when it comes to food, as well as all the various flavors that exist. Among these activities are baking or cooking with you to guide them, trying out foods they've never had before, or taking part in games involving taste to help your child develop a more complex palate.

Smell sensory play obviously works with your child's sense of smell. You can teach your child about the various aromas and scents that exist. You can work with herbs or spices, toddler-safe perfumes, slime, scented play dough, etc. You can also craft games based on smell where your child has to guess what it is they're smelling.

Sensory Activities

1. **Rainbow Rice Sensory Bin:** For this activity, you'll need a large container that you fill with different colors of rice. You should also provide your toddler with cups, scoops, and other small toys. The cups and scoops are meant to help your toddlers scoop up some rice and pour it. All the various toys are to be hidden within the container of rice so that your toddler can feel around for them. This will work on both your toddler's sense of touch and sight.

2. **Scented Playdough:** You can scent your playdough using food extracts or essential oils. Make sure that these materials are safe for your toddler to interact with. They can have fun shaping and squeezing the dough. This would engage their sense of smell and touch while helping them develop various skills.

Watermelon Kool Aid Play Dough Recipe

Scented watermelon playdough is easy to make and such fun watermelon activities for kids of all ages! Use in watermelon theme or summer play. (Not for Consumption)

Equipment

> 2 large bowls
> stove top to heat water

Ingredients

1 packet Watermelon Kool-aid unsweetened drink mix
1 cup flour
1/2 cup salt
1 cup water
2 Tablespoons cream of tartar
1 Tablespoons Vegetable Oil, or similar

Ingredients

1. Commence by blending all the dry components (excluding the kool-aid) in a spacious bowl.
2. Proceed to bring the water to a boil on medium heat. Once it's boiling, transfer it to a bowl and introduce the oil.
3. Integrate the amalgamated dry components. Should it remain sticky after thorough blending, consider adding roughly 1/4 cup of flour incrementally. Let it cool for 5-10 minutes or until manageable.
4. Upon reaching a manageable temperature, divide the kool-aid playdough into two portions. Approximately 1/4 of the dough will represent the watermelon rind, while the remaining 3/4 will form the succulent red fruit. To avoid getting your hands messy, utilize a ziplock bag for food coloring. Apply green food dye to the smaller portion and mix.
5. Embed dry black beans into the red section to mimic seeds. Indulge in the joy of molding and playing with this entertaining watermelon-themed activity!

3. **Bubble Wrap Stomp:** With this activity, you only need a sheet or two of bubble wrap. Allow your toddler to jump and stomp on the bubbles barefoot to pop them. If they want, they can also pop the bubbles with their fingers.

4. **Sensory Nature Walks:** Take your toddler on a nature walk, but this time, the goal is to encourage them to touch everything they can as long as it's safe. Be mindful of such things as poison ivy. Have your toddler also pay attention to the various sounds of nature around them as well as different smells.

5. **Sensory Balloon Play:** This activity requires grabbing some balloons and filling them with rice, sand, or water. Allow your toddlers to enjoy squeezing and rolling the balloons, paying attention to the various weights and textures of each one.

6. **Sensory Sound Shakers:** For this, you need some small containers and fill them with such things as bells, beans, rice, and some sand. Have your toddler shake each of these containers and pay attention to the various sounds that are produced. By having your toddler do this, you teach them to discriminate between sounds, understand rhythm, and develop their fine motor skills.

7. **Taste Exploration:** This sensory play involves having your toddler taste appropriate foods for their age. You should have bitter, salty, sour, savory, and sweet things. You should have your toddler pay attention to how the food tastes and how it feels in their mouth.

8. **Sensory Painting:** Give your toddler various materials they can use to paint, such as sponges, feathers, or various objects of different textures. Encourage them to notice the differences in the textures and how the textures affect the kind of patterns that they can create with these objects.

9. **Sensory Water Play:** Provide your toddler with various containers of water with different objects of different sizes. They should also vary in terms of the shapes and textures of these objects. Have your toddler pour the water, splash around, and feel what it's like as they explore the objects within them. This way, you will improve their tactile sensation, hand-eye coordination, and much more.

10. **Ice Chipping:** For this activity, you will take some of your toddler's toys, put them in some water, and then freeze them. When they're nice and frozen, you can set your toddler up with some safe hammers so they can break the ice. Make sure that your toddler is old enough to do this safely and that you do not leave them unsupervised. It's very satisfying for them to chip away at the ice. This will offer them better hand-eye coordination, an understanding of their strength, and satisfaction when they finally get at the toy. They can also enjoy safely exploring what cold feels like.

11. **Sensory Optical Course:** You're going to create an obstacle course using all kinds of fun materials like throw pillows, textured mats, balance beams, and tunnels. Allow your toddler to climb, crawl, twist, and turn through this course. In the process, your toddler will work with their tactile sense and learn how to move their body.

12. **Sensory Sock Bin:** Grab a bin and fill it up with socks of different textures, such as silky socks, ripped ones, fuzzy ones, and so on. Get your toddler to feel around in this bin so that they can explore the various textures. Not only can they touch them, but they can also stretch the fabrics. You can also get them to sort them out based on the way they feel.

13. **Sensory Hide and Seek:** For this exercise, you're going to hide little objects or toys in a sensory bin that's filled with other stuff like shredded paper, dried beans, or rice. Your toddler needs to dig through these materials to discover the items you've hidden.

14. **Sensory Water Beads**: Grab a container and fill it with water beads. Let your toddler have fun enjoying the squishiness of these beads and their vibrant colors. Let them pour, scoop, and transfer the beads however they want to, using their hands, cups, spoons, and other tools.

15. **Sensory Sound Walk:** Take your toddler on a walk around the block or your neighborhood. As you walk, encourage them to pay attention to the various sounds around them, such as their footsteps. Let them pay attention to what it sounds like when walking on gravel versus on grass or pavement. Get them to also feel what it's like with their shoes on one surface versus another.

16. **Bubble Wrap Painting:** Set up large sheets of bubble wrap to serve as canvases for your little one to paint on. Make sure you provide them with washable, non-toxic paint. Demonstrate how interesting this can be by showing them what happens when you pop the bubbles after painting, as it creates unique textures and patterns. This lovely activity will encourage your little one to be more creative.

17. **Sensory Story Time**: Choose one of your toddler's favorite story books, which has loads of sensory elements, like pop-ups, interactive parts, textures, and so on. Read it to them and allow them to explore and interact with the various sensations of the book.

18. **Sensory Garden:** You can create a sensory garden of sorts for your little one by getting together materials like flower petals, soft grass, smooth rocks, and scented flowers. Put them in a play area. Encourage your child to go around the garden touching, smelling, and observing the different colors and textures of each item.

19. **Sensory Obstacle Course**: You can set up an obstacle course, but this time, use materials that have very different textures, colors, and so on. Whatever you choose to include as part of the obstacle course, it's got to be something that will not hurt your child or make them find it boring. You should encourage your toddler to overcome the obstacle course and take their time exploring the various sensations and sights around them. You can also use auditory cues to make the activity even more engaging for them.

20. **Musical Charades:** Play different clips of music that represent various emotions. Play a little bit and then ask them to express what they felt as they listened to the music. If you have safe musical videos for your little one to watch, you can also play those for them and have them communicate the emotions the singers appear to be feeling.

21. **Bedtime Sing-Along**: This is a great way to have a calming routine to get your toddler to wind down for the day. It's a great activity that will help them relax and feel secure. You can just sing a song or lullaby and get your toddler to sing along with you.

Tips for Safe and Engaging Sensory Play

- Always pick material that is safe and age-appropriate for your toddler. You should avoid small objects that could be choking hazards and always look for non-toxic materials.

- You must always be nearby to closely supervise your child. Pay attention to their actions; when needed, you should intervene to keep them from ingesting materials they shouldn't or to stop an accident from happening.

- You must create a designated space for sensory play. This should be an area where your child can play and explore safely and where they understand that boundaries should not be crossed. This will help you clean up more easily when they're done.

- You must also set boundaries in the form of ground rules. Let your toddler know what's okay for them to do, and clearly express the guidelines they need to follow.

- When working with your toddler on sensory play, make sure you're using a sensory tray or a bin. This way, you contain the area in which they play, and it's easier for them to have fun exploring the various materials you've provided.

- Think about their sensory preferences. The way to do this is to pay attention to what your child prefers. You'll know this based on the toys or materials that they tend to ignore during the sessions. In their next session, provide them with the colors, textures, sounds, senses, and tastes you know they prefer.

- Consider every sense your child has and look for materials to engage and stimulate them. You can combine music with some tactile materials.

- When your child is done with sensory play, you must always follow up with something that would calm them. This is because sensory play can be very stimulating. Therefore, consider getting your child to read a book, engage in cuddle time, or play some quiet music so that they can relax once more.

Chapter 7: Play and Socialization

This chapter will show the importance of play and encouraging social skills in your toddler.

Theoretical Perspectives on Play and Socialization

The Social Learning Theory: According to this theory, when it comes to learning and socialization, what matters the most is observation and behavior modeling. In other words, children tend to look around them to observe other people's behavior and then mimic those behaviors. This is how your child learns about the various social roles and expectations that exist.

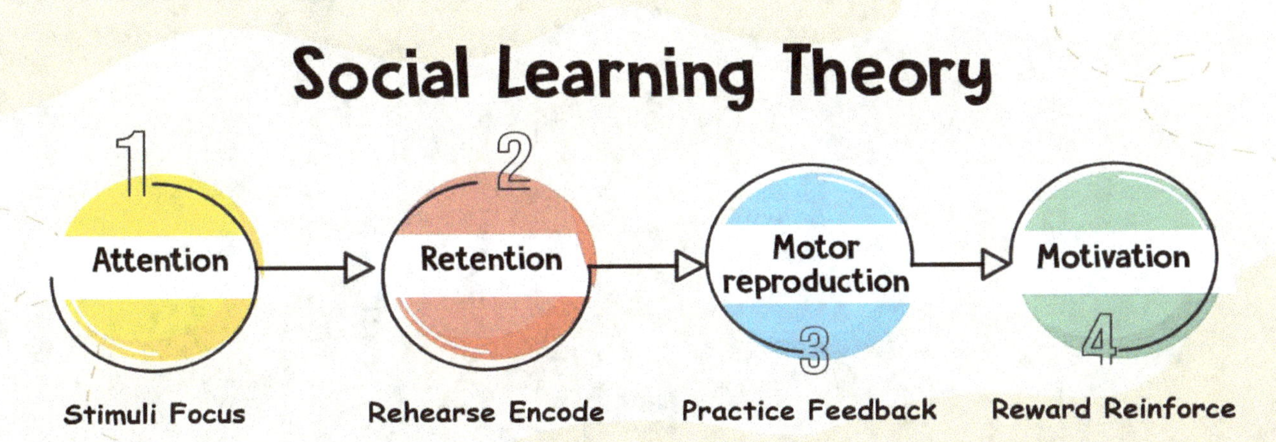

The Cognitive Developmental Theory: This theory focuses on how much play matters when it comes to a child's development and how it is connected to their ability to socialize. This theory suggests that through play, your child will be able to understand how the world functions and have the social skills necessary to connect with their peers.

The Social-Cultural Theory: This theory is about the cultural and social influences your child is exposed to and how these affect how your child plays and socializes. According to this theory, play is essential for developing cognitive and social skills.

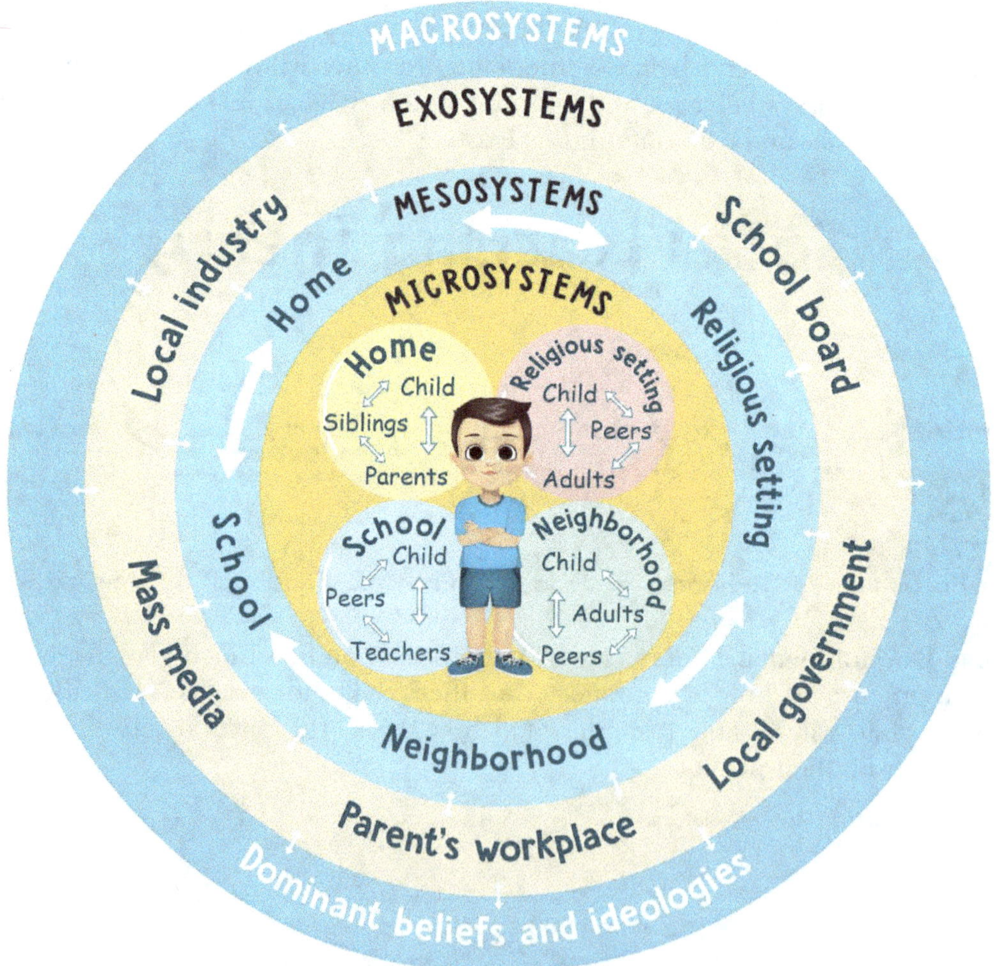

Symbolic Interactionism: This theory is also heavily centered around play in terms of symbolism. Symbolic play is all about working with various objects and specific actions to represent other things. Your child will be able to practice various social rules, roles, and languages. It's about working with their imagination so they can internalize these things and use them in their real-life experiences.

Ecological Systems Theory: This theory is about how peers, the community, and the child's immediate family can work together to influence how they play and socialize.

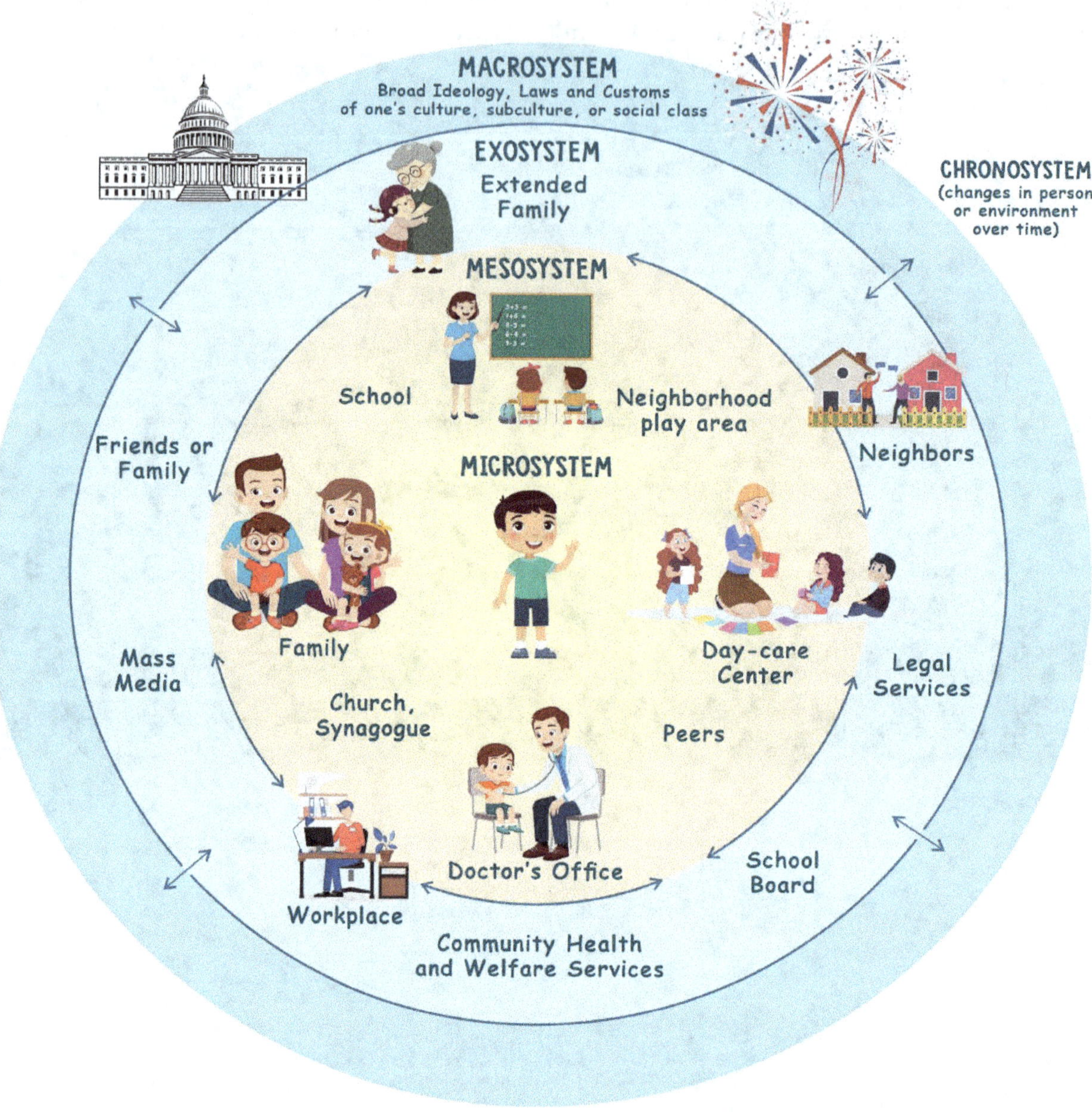

Cultural-Historical Theory: This theory is about the social-cultural influences that affect your child's ability to play and socialize and the historical influences that have led to this present point. It's about the importance of various tools of culture, such as playing materials and language, in helping your child mediate their interactions with others and how they learn about life.

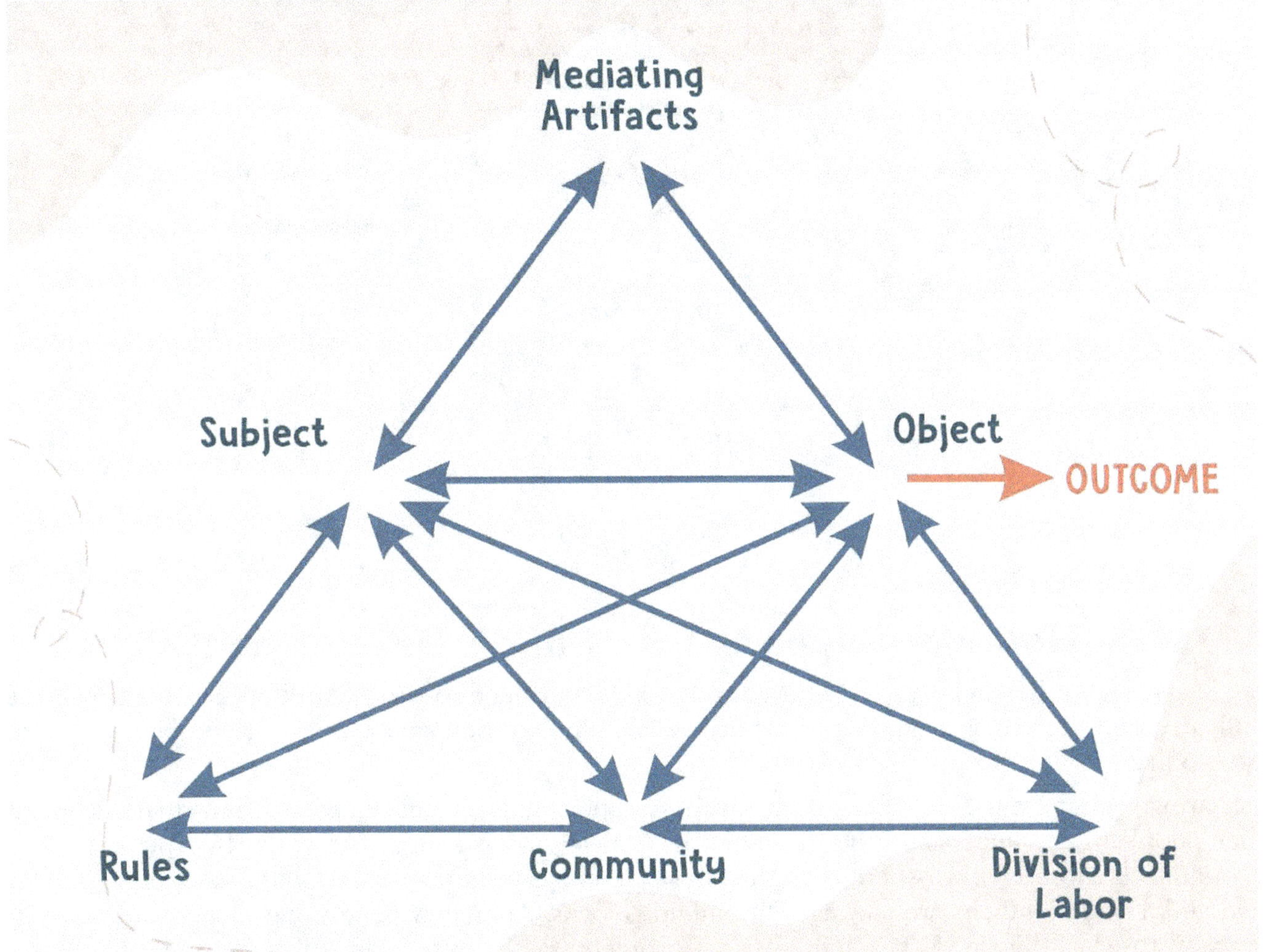

The Self-Determination Theory: This one is about the intrinsic desires and the sense of autonomy that your child has when it comes to playing and socialization. According to this theory, when your child is engaged in play activities that align with their desires and allowed to be a competent individual, your child will experience the very best situation for social development. All of these theories provide different perspectives that you could use to understand the ideas of playing and socialization and how they affect your child's life.

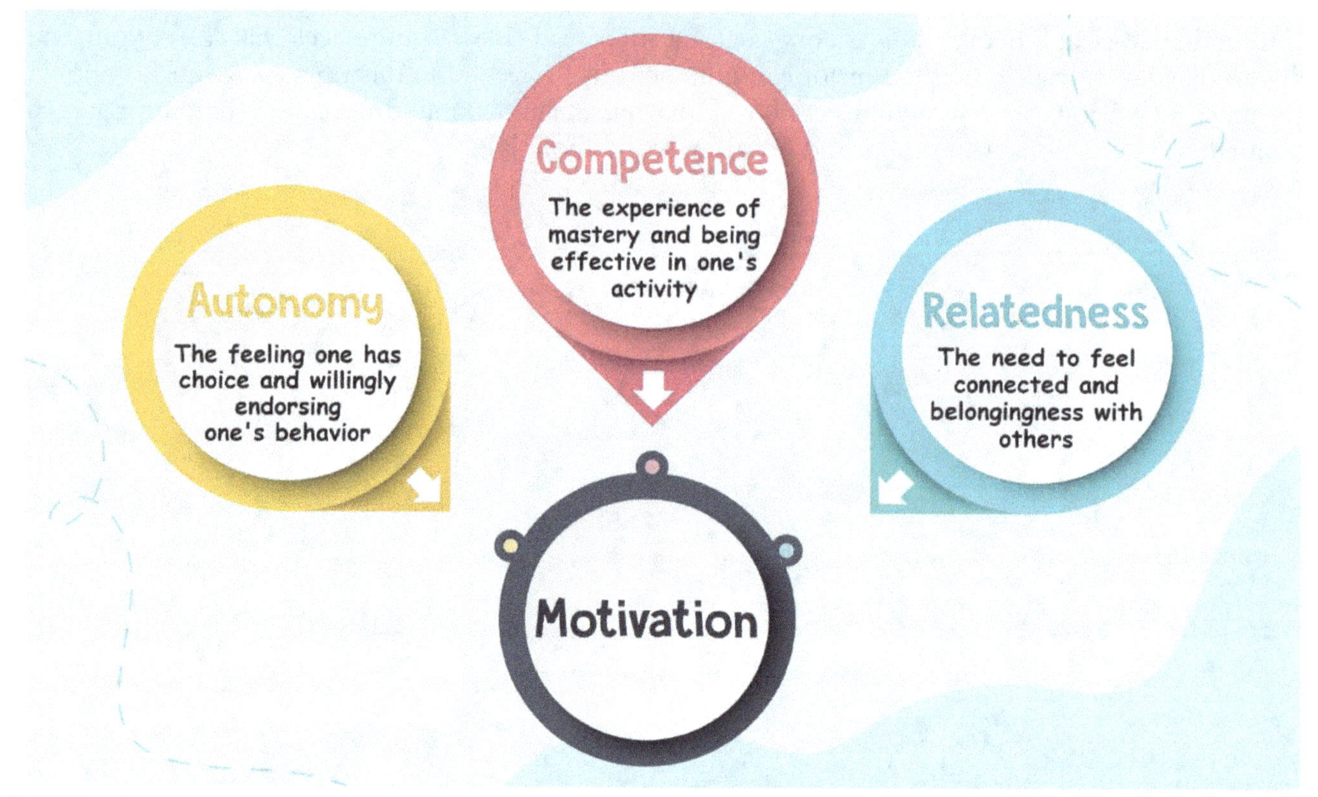

How Play Supports Your Child's Development

Play is essential to helping your child develop the skills they need to survive in life, such as cooperation, conflict resolution, and sharing. Here is a very detailed look at how you can use play to help your child develop these skills.

Sharing: When your child plays, they have the opportunity to practice what it means to share with other people. They understand the importance of having to take turns. As your child plays, they will encounter certain scenarios where they must share their toys, other materials, or roles. Imagine your child and a friend of theirs are playing with building blocks. They may need to negotiate whose turn it is to play with which blocks. When they play with someone else, your child will understand these things and learn to think about other people's perspectives and wants.

Cooperation: Play is also a great way to encourage a child to work with others to achieve a specific aim. When you and your child work together, or when your child cooperates with others in play, your child learns the importance of collaborating. They understand they cannot just take their opinions and feelings and lord them over everyone else. Your child learns to communicate effectively and to listen to what others are actually saying to them, as well as the importance of coordination.

For instance, imagine your child is part of a group of children who are working together to create a fort on the playground. Obviously, each of these children will have certain tasks they must perform, they will have to share ideas, and they must be supportive of one another if they intend to actually build that for its success. By cooperatively playing with others, your child will learn how to work as part of a team to solve problems and how to effectively communicate their wants and needs.

Conflict Resolution: The great thing about playing is that your child has a safe environment in which they can learn about conflict and how to resolve it. As children play with one another, it's natural for conflicts to come up. These are often over who gets to share what, whose ideas should be implemented, or which goal matters most. Imagine your child and another are in disagreement over which game to play next. They can both learn to negotiate and compromise and work up a mutually satisfying solution. For instance, your child may agree to take turns to play each game or come up with a different game that they both want to play right away. Through the avenue of play, your child will learn how to deal with various conflicts and come up with various strategies for resolution, such as expressing how they feel, actively listening to the other person to understand them better, making compromises, or seeking guidance from others more competent or grown-up when required.

Perspective Taking: Your child needs to learn how to take on other people's perspectives if they're going to have a chance to develop empathy and understand other people's feelings. There's no better way to accomplish this than through play. Using imaginative play, for instance, your child can take on all sorts of roles and pretend to be someone else, which would allow them to see life from other perspectives besides their limited view. Your child and others may decide to play doctor or house, and together, they can come up with different situations, allowing them to relate more easily to the feelings and perspectives of other people.

Following Rules: Play is an excellent tool to teach your younger one the importance of following rules. Society would fall apart if there were no rules. Therefore, by using play, you can teach a little one how to stick to the rules and why they should. Playing games centered around rules will teach your little one the importance of being fair to others and not breaking any rules. You can engage your little one in a board game that has various rules and involves taking turns. This has the added advantage of teaching your child the importance of patience.

Solving Problems: Playing is a great way to enhance your child's ability to solve problems as they deal with the challenges and conflicts that arise as they play with their peers. Your child will learn how to spot a problem when it crops up, brainstorm to figure out a way around it – and take stock of the results of their chosen actions. For instance, imagine your child is part of a group working on creating a bridge with building blocks, but the blocks keep collapsing. Your child and other children may then decide that it would be best to try a different approach. They know they have to devise a different strategy and work together as a team to solve the problem. As your child plays, they'll learn it is okay to try things and have them not work out how they expected. By learning they won't always get things right, they discover they can think creatively to solve problems, and they can critically analyze what they did wrong so they can get it right *the next time.* It also teaches them that there is no reason to feel bad just because they came up with a solution that hasn't worked. They just have to try something else. These are all the ways in which play can help your child in social interactions, cooperation, and negotiation with others.

Activities

1. **Pretend Play:** Engage your toddler in imaginative scenarios like playing doctor, house, running a restaurant, managing a school, and so on. By playing this way, you encourage your child to interact with others socially, learn to negotiate and communicate with others, and so on.

2. **Cooperative Board Games**: Invest in getting board games that require your toddler to work with others.

MEMORY GAME

Print twice and cut out the cards

HELP THE BEAR GET TO THE BERRIES
20 21 22 23 24 25 26 27
19
18 17 16 15 14 13 12 11 10
9
1 2 3 4 5 6 7 8

HELP THE GIRL GO THROUH THE JUNGLE
23 24 26 27 FINISH
22
& go up
25
go back
21 19 18
20
go back
13 17
12 14
go back
15 16
11
10
& go up
9 8 7 6
go up
5
START 1 2
& go up
3 4

3. **Construction Challenges**: Get your toddler to work with others. You should provide them with Lego blocks, magnetic tiles, etc. You can then ask them to create something such as a car, bridge, or the tallest tower they can.

4. **Team Sports**: You can have your toddler participate in team sports, allowing them to learn the value of communicating with others and cooperating. Some of the best sports to consider would be soccer, baseball, basketball, or even relay races.

5. **Collaborative Art**: There's no reason your toddler should make art on their own. You can get other toddlers to join with them. Consider such things as collage making, mirror painting, or group sculpting.

6. **Pictionary**: Charades and Pictionary are excellent ways to allow your child to communicate with others and work to understand them. The great thing about these games is that they involve working with nonverbal cues and finding creative ways to express yourself.

7. **Puppet Shows**: You can have your child perform puppet shows with you or other children. Let them improvise. This will allow them to be creative and interact with others. You'll also teach your child inadvertently about character development, telling stories, and performing with others.

8. **Group Science Experiments**: Getting your child to cooperate with other children is a fantastic way to ensure they'll have no problems finding their feet socially the older they get. Using group science experiments is a fun, efficient way to teach your child how to get along with others, so get them involved as often as you can. Encourage your child to use their skills of observation. You can have them work with other small groups of children and carry out simple experiments such as mixing colors to see what they'll get, testing the various properties of water, and so on.

9. **Set Up Team Building Challenges**: An example would be building a bridge using limited materials. You can challenge the children to try solving a puzzle within a given time limit. This would encourage your child to work with other children to figure out the problem as quickly as possible.

10. **Circle Time**: This activity involves having children sit together in a circle to share stories, experiences they've had, or other things they enjoy with others in the group. The idea behind this is to foster listening skills, get your little one to interact with others, and actively understand what others are sharing.

Strategies to Support Social Play

Try Guided Role-Play. This is a great way for you to encourage your child to develop socially. You can offer your child various scenarios, themes, and props to play with others. You could create a pretend grocery store and have the children take on various roles so that they can communicate and negotiate with each other. One child may play the manager, another the cashier, another a shopper, and so on.

Model Appropriate Behavior. As the adult in the room, you must act in a way your little one can copy. Along with other adults, try to demonstrate to your child how to communicate effectively, share with others, take turns, and resolve any issues that may arise. You can do this by modeling how to actively listen, solve problems, and respectfully communicate disagreements with others.

Encourage Cooperative Playtime. As often as possible, always set up situations where your child can play cooperatively with others. This is essential if you want to give them a shot at being a social master.

So, sign your child up for any events or activities that will require them to collaborate with others, empathize with their peers, and work as a team to make decisions.

Chapter 8: Music and Emotional Regulation

When it comes to emotional regulation, music can have a profound effect. This chapter shows the power of music and how it can help your toddler handle their emotions.

The Connection Between Music and Emotions

Have you ever listened to a piece of music and felt like it moved your core? Good music will do that to you, as it takes you to beautiful heights and depths of emotion, helping you explore your inner landscape. It moves you. It has the power to evoke feelings you didn't even know you had. It can even impact your emotional well-being and change the way you perceive life. Music has the ability to influence your emotions because it directly influences certain parts of your brain involved in the processing of emotion, including the hippocampus, amygdala, and prefrontal cortex.

When it comes to play therapy for your toddler, music is a tool that you can use to help your child recognize their emotions and express them. For instance, when your child is encouraged to listen to all sorts of music to figure out the various feelings each piece evokes, you are essentially teaching them how to handle their emotions. You're teaching them that depending on what they're listening to, they may feel a certain way. You can even encourage your child to try to create their own music as an outlet to express the way that they feel.

Music can help your child recognize and express emotions.

Music can help your child to develop their emotional and social skills. Engaging your child in certain musical activities involving other people, such as playing instruments as a group or singing in a choir, can help your child learn about the power of communicating with others, cooperating, and developing empathy. It is also a great way to offer your child a shared emotional experience and the feeling of being connected to other people. The human experience is one that is founded on the principle "no man is an island," implying everyone is a social creature, no matter how introverted or reclusive they are. Music, therefore, is a great unifier that can solidify the bonds your child forms with people around them.

Music is so powerful that some World War II veterans in the United States were treated using music therapy. This form of therapy had very effective results on people who struggled with traumatic brain injury, neurological conditions, and psychological issues like PTSD.

Music and Mood

The fact that music can serve as an excellent way to improve mental health is not a new thing. It's been known for several thousands of years. Think about ancient philosophers like Confucius and Plato or the kings of Israel who understood the importance of singing praises to deal with stress. Even now, military bands use music in order to boost the morale and courage of the soldiers. When you're watching any sporting event, you'll notice that there's music playing in order to make the crowds and the players more enthusiastic about what's about to happen. In schools, children work with music to help them memorize certain concepts or the alphabet. Go to a shopping mall, and you notice that the kind of music that plays is meant to lull you into a sense of comfort and make you not want to leave the store. Go to the dentist's office, and you'll notice there's some music playing to help nervous patients calm down.

Genres and Effects

There is a plethora of musical genres, and having so many options makes sense when you consider differences in personal taste, culture, the emotional tone of each genre, etc. Yet, in spite of these differences in musical genres, there are certain universal responses. Babies really enjoy the sound of a lullaby. A mother singing to her child is a very soothing thing, regardless of whether the mother has a great voice or not. There are particular genres of music that make people feel terrible even when they claim to enjoy it. In a study of 144 adults and teenagers who were made to listen to four different sorts of music, of all the genres, grunge music was the worst in terms of its effects on people. It led to a rise in hostility, made people even sadder than they were, increased tension, and caused the entire group to feel fatigued. This was the case even for the teenagers who claimed they enjoyed grunge. In another study, college students who listened to pop, rock, and classical music said that only the former made them feel optimistic about life and even made them a lot happier.

Music is also excellent for helping those who struggle with anxiety. If your toddler is anxious, you can play something relaxing. Relaxing music can regulate their emotions and improve their cognitive abilities when they're throwing a tantrum. There have been studies that suggest that music is excellent for handling depression as well. You don't have to be depressed, nor does your toddler, to enjoy music's uplifting effect. It's great for treating those with medical conditions and illnesses like burns and cancer, too; for this reason, it only makes sense that if your toddler is throwing a tantrum or struggling to grasp a concept, you can simply play some calming music for them.

Music and Memory

Another great thing about music is that it's much easier for you to remember things if you put them in a song. Music has been known to enhance your memory and recall. It is especially great for children and adolescents who struggle with attention problems. You can use it to reward them for acting in the way you'd like them to. If your toddler pays attention to something serious, like their homework, for about five to ten minutes, you may reward them with a chance to listen to some fun music for just about five minutes.

Music for Focus

You can even work with songs, interesting rhythms, and even dance to help those who struggle to focus. Working with baroque music is excellent for improving reasoning and attention. If a student is playing background music, it's not distracting for them and could help them focus as long as the music has no lyrics. You can also use musical cues to help your little one tell when it is time for one activity or another. Finally, when you play calming music, you encourage open, outgoing, and social behavior. You reduce the possibility of being impulsive.

Musical Activities

1. **Soothing Lullabies:** You don't have to be an opera singer to pull this off. If you can't sing, all you have to do is play soft lullabies to calm and soothe your toddler. There's no lovelier way to bond with your toddler than when it's time for them to hit the hay at the end of the day, and you need them to calm down because they're feeling stressed or throwing tantrums.

2. **Musical Breathing:** For this activity, you must guide your toddler to take deep breaths while playing calming instrumental music. You can model how they should breathe by showing them what to do. Factor in how deeply they're able to breathe, as they may not be able to take as deep a breath as you can. Make sure you're both breathing in sync with the music, as this is a great way for you both to relax and even increase your bond.

3. **Sensory Shakers:** Whip out the little handheld shakers and give them to your toddler. Your shaker can be full of stuff like beads, beans, rice, or dried pasta broken into pieces. Next, you're going to shake them in various rhythms. Then, get your toddler to copy. Choose rhythms that are easy to emulate. This will help them develop a sense of rhythm and calm them down.

4. **Expressive Dance:** You can show your toddler how to move, sway, or dance freely to the music they choose. This is a great way for you to work with them when they're throwing too many tantrums. They may have a lot of pent-up energy that they need to release. Moving is a great way to express those emotions and help them regulate their feelings.

5. **Exploring Instruments:** You should get a few child-friendly instruments and allow your toddler to explore them. Allow them to play however they want, no matter how bad it sounds. It doesn't matter if they're making actual music. The point here is to get them to explore the various possible sounds.

6. **Stories with Music:** Tell your toddler stories while you have some music in the backdrop. Make sure to choose music that matches the theme of the story you want to tell so you can enhance their engagement. With time, you may point out to your toddler how the music made the story more dramatic or interesting by trying to tell the story again without the music. This is a great way

to teach them that they can emotionally regulate with music.

7. **Dancing with Scarves:** Give your toddler a few colorful scarves, and play some music at different tempos. You should get them to move freely and express themselves by playing with the scarves.

8. **Musical Mirroring:** You and your toddler need to stand face-to-face. Then, while playing some music, make random dance moves and let them imitate you.

9. **Hunting for Sounds:** This exercise involves you and your toddler going around the home or outdoors to listen carefully and try to figure out the different sounds. Among the ones to look out for are the sound of the fridge humming, water running, birds chirping, trees moving, distant music or traffic, and so on. This is a great way to encourage your toddler to become more aware of their surroundings and the sounds in them.

10. **Musical Yoga:** If your toddler is old enough to control their body, you can practice some yoga with music playing in the background. The music should be soft instrumentals, and you can guide them through easy stretches. This will help them to become more aware of their body and relax even further.

11. **Writing Songs:** They don't have to be masterpieces. They just need to be written by both of you. Encourage your toddler to share their input and create melodies or lyrics based on the things that they have experienced and what they're feeling.

12. **Music and Puppet Play:** You can play some music while your toddler works with puppets to act out various stories or songs. You can switch through different songs with different moods so your toddler can change the story to match the song. By playing with puppets and using music to tell stories, you get your child to notice the structure inherent in storytelling, which means they'll get better at this skill with time.

13. **Name the Tune:** This is a lovely, fun one where you get to play snippets of songs that your toddler is familiar with and encourage them to guess the name of the song. This is a great way to get your toddler to be able to recognize sounds easily and improve their memory and knowledge of music.

14. **The Singing Ball:** In this exercise, you and your toddler can sit opposite each other or in a circle with other people. Ideally, you should have a soft ball. Pass it back and forth or around the circle as you sing a song together. This is a great way to encourage your toddler to learn the importance of waiting their turn, interacting with others, and enjoying time with others.

15. **Musical Hide and Seek:** For this game, hide a toy somewhere in the room and then play some music to help your toddler find the object. The closer they get, the louder the music should get. The further away they are from the object, the quieter it gets. This is a great way to encourage them to pay attention to what they hear, get better at spatial awareness, and solve problems.

16. **Transitional Music:** Work with music that is rhythmic and upbeat to encourage your toddler to be excited. This is the kind of music you should play to start the day. By using music to mark when it's time to switch to a different activity, you'll reduce the odds of them arguing with you or getting fussy about having to stop whatever they're doing. Music is also an excellent tool for grabbing your little one's attention, so that's a bonus you can take advantage of.

17. **Create a Mood-Based Playlist:** You should have a playlist of songs for certain moods. Take the time to curate a playlist that will have various effects on your toddler, like getting them hyped up or calming them down.

18. **Musical Freeze Dance:** You will need to play some energetic music. The idea here is to get your toddler to dance however they want, no matter how goofy it looks. Every now and then, you're going to pause the music, and when you do, they will need to freeze in a pose. This way, you'll be teaching them how to listen, control themselves, and regulate their emotions.

19. **Singing Feelings:** When your toddler feels down or excited, you can get them to sing about their feelings. Certain songs already address these different emotions, such as "If You're Happy and You Know It" or "If You're Angry and You Know It." Alternatively, you can get your toddler to freestyle and just sing about how they feel. You don't need them to sing a particular melody, as the goal is to just let them do what they can and have fun with the game. It is a good idea for you to model this first to give them the confidence to copy you.

20. **Drum Release:** If you offer your toddler some drums or percussive instruments, you can get them to let go of whatever negative feelings they're having. Banging on drums is a great way to get rid of pent-up anger, frustration, and tension. On top of that, they'll have so much fun that they end up tiring themselves out in the end.

21. **Relaxation Time**: This activity involves playing calming, soothing music. The music should not have any lyrics that will distract your toddler and make them excited or agitated. You may want to play these when it's time to relax or calm down. Or, you can help them focus on their homework or whatever activity it is they're doing by playing this relaxing music.

22. **Emotional Humming**: This is almost like singing feelings, except that, in this case, you are going to encourage your toddler to hum to express how they're feeling at the moment. So, first, get your toddler to identify the emotion they have before humming about it. As usual, you should first model the behavior so they know what to do.

Chapter 9: Evaluating Progress and Overcoming Challenges

The Importance of Regular Progress Assessment

You should regularly assess your child's progress when it comes to play therapy. You must understand that for your child, play therapy is a great therapeutic outlet that helps your child communicate and express themselves just as they're naturally inclined to. Play therapy is a safe and supportive way for your child to explore their various emotions and take responsibility for their actions. Not only that, but play therapy will also help your child solve their problems more efficiently.

You must realize that as a parent, you have a very important part to play in supporting your child's progress. You can't just hand over your child to the therapist and expect that everything will work out. You must be actively involved, and part of that means you must regularly check in on their progress.

Progress assessments can help you see how your child is developing.

Give yourself some homework: To learn about your child and study them as you would study a new subject you don't understand yet. The more you learn about your little bundle of joy, the more you'll understand how to connect with them and foster feelings of trust so your relationship is rock solid. Your therapist will start the session without your child because they must connect with you first. They will listen to the various concerns that you have so they can gain some insight into what your child is struggling with and better understand the dynamics of your family.

The next thing is that you must discuss the objectives and goals you are interested in with your therapist. You can't just start without any clear goal in mind. You need to be able to assess how effective the sessions are for your child, and that means figuring out the objectives that you would like to accomplish with your child right from the start. The various goals that you may be concerned with include helping your child become more self-reliant, more confident, better able to accept themselves, better at solving problems and taking responsibility, and so on. Whatever your goals are, they must be measurable, concrete, and observable.

The next thing to expect is for the therapist to explain to you how their behavior in the playroom can help your child accomplish the goals you would like them to. The therapist should clearly explain to you how your child's decision-making process and their ability to control themselves in the playroom will eventually be observed in their attitude outside of the therapy sessions.

Tracking your child's progress with play therapy also means that there must be ongoing consultations. You cannot expect to see changes in just a day or a week of working with your therapist. Every four or five sessions, your therapist checks in with you so that you can both be aware of what progress, if any, your child is making. This way, your therapist will know if they need to make any adjustments in their approach to helping your child achieve the objectives you have set for them. The therapist can also let you know where you may be going wrong and help you adjust.

Challenges to Contend with and How to Overcome Them

You may have to face certain challenges when working with your child to accomplish the goals you have in mind for them. For one thing, you may have to contend with delayed development. You see, some children who take part in play therapy may not develop as quickly as their peers in certain other aspects, such as social skills, language, or regulating emotions. It doesn't necessarily mean that there's something wrong with your child, and you should definitely not make them feel that way. You must understand that the delayed development can make it more challenging for your child to be fully engaged in play therapy. A good therapist would be aware of these delays and would do their best to adjust their methods as needed. Maybe they need to offer simpler instructions for your child to follow. Maybe they need to be more supportive. They may just have to adjust the activities in a way that matches your child. Whether you're a parent or therapist, you must meet the child halfway so they can actually grow and develop.

Another challenge you may deal with is resistance to certain activities. Some children are simply averse to certain activities. It could be because they're afraid, uncomfortable, or just not interested. Your therapist needs to work out why your child is reacting the way they are, and not only that, you must both be respectful of your child's boundaries. If you notice that your child continues to refuse to take part in certain activities, the therapist has to figure out an alternative method or introduce a different activity that's meant to achieve the same results. This way, you develop their trust and make them feel much safer. They will eventually understand that the environment they're in is free of both judgment and criticism. When they realize that, there is a chance they will circle back to the activities they refused to take part in at first.

Sometimes, your child's emotions may be incredibly difficult to manage. Play therapy is all about exploring the different emotions and how they can express them. Even for adults, emotions are challenging. Your child may struggle with trying to figure out what they're feeling, let alone why they're feeling it. On top of that, they may have trouble containing their emotional responses to certain things and explaining how they feel the way they do. Your therapist has to do everything they can to support your child to help them handle the whirlwind of emotions. To do this, your child has to have a safe space to express themselves. You and the therapist must do whatever you can to validate your child's feelings and offer guidance by modeling healthy coping strategies. In the end, they will learn how to communicate what they feel. But you must be patient with them and resist the urge to rush the process.

No one should ever consider all children to be the same, as certain approaches that work for one may not work for another. However, there are certain strategies that tend to work across the board. For one thing, you and the therapist must be flexible and adaptable in your approach. Whatever you do must be tailored to your child's needs and capabilities.

This should go without saying when trying to accomplish things with children, but patience and empathy are absolutely necessary. Children are very sensitive, and they can pick up on when you're irritated or dissatisfied. Having them feel like a burden will only hinder, or even cancel out, any progress you made so far.

Another thing to remember is that the parents and the therapist need to cooperate when handling the issues surrounding the child's life. By doing so, your therapist would be able to see things you may not have noticed before and recommend ways you can be more supportive of your child outside of therapy sessions.

When you engage with your child, you need to be playful at times. The best way to get your little one engaged in the activity is to tailor the experiences to what they prefer and keep their interests in mind. Your therapist will suggest new toys, games, and activities based on your answers to their questions at your first session.

Finally, the therapist you choose must be one who is open to self-reflection and constant supervision. This therapist, ideally, checks in with other therapists to process their experience as they work with your child, to receive new insights, and, where needed, refine their strategy toward helping your child accomplish the goals you set out at the start of your sessions.

Tracking Your Child's Progress

The following is a comprehensive guide to help you track your little one's developmental progress.

1. **Use traditional pen and paper.** You can journal at the end of each day. Write down your observations about your child's behavior. Note any milestones they've hit, challenges they may face, and behaviors they exhibit. Use a calendar to mark the important events or milestones your child hits. A calendar is an excellent tool to visualize their progress over time.

2. **Use digital apps.** You can use spreadsheets like Google Sheets or Excel to track various skills and behaviors your child is exhibiting. Create different categories for these behaviors. Log their observations each week or day using various colors and symbols to show how much progress they're making. Chart their progress with a graph or apps for tracking child development.

3. **Work with behavioral charts.** Whenever your child behaves how you'd like them to, give them a sticker and put it on their chart for them to see. This is a visual way to encourage them to do well each time. Also, develop a behavioral point system. Anytime your child does something well, they get a point. When they've accumulated a set amount of points, you reward them.

4. **Use visual aids.** Take photographs of your child whenever they have accomplished something huge. Photograph their projects, art, and new activities that they're involved in. With time, their development will be evident to you and them. Milestone boxes are also a handy tool. Get a box and put different items such as the first letter they wrote you, their art, and anything significant they have created.

5. **Use standardized testing.** If your child is of school age, test them periodically with a standardized test to see their academic performance.

6. **Get feedback from others.** The people giving you feedback should be trustworthy. Get regular updates from coaches, teachers, tutors, and instructors your child interacts with. This will give you a balanced external perspective and ensure you are not missing something because of how close you are to your child. Feedback can include what other children have to say about your child.

7. **Self-assessment works.** Try using a progress booklet where your child can write or draw whatever they've learned or accomplished each week. This is a great way to encourage them to learn how to self-reflect and become more self-aware. Set a regular time when you and your child can talk about how they feel, what they feel proud of accomplishing, and the obstacles they're facing.

8. **Try structured observation.** While your child plays, observe them. Don't interrupt. Pay attention to any new behaviors they exhibit or new skills they pick up. You may assign them tasks, such as a puzzle, and see how they solve it.

9. **Work with checklists and inventories.** You can create developmental milestone checklists that are age-appropriate. As your child hits each milestone, tick it off. The same applies to behavioral checklists. Pay attention to the skills and behaviors you would like your child to exhibit more, and note when and how they act as you'd prefer.

10. **Use professional evaluation.** Have a pediatrician regularly check up on your child to ensure their physical health is as it should be. Work with counselors or therapists regularly to see how your child is progressing.

These are ways to track your child's progress as you work with them. Remember, you should never compare your child to another. Be as objective as possible regardless of how emotionally involved you are. Whenever there's progress, no matter how little, celebrate it.

If you notice a method of tracking your child's progress isn't working for you, it's okay to change it. You can always tweak these methods to create something that works for you and your baby. The goal of tracking their progress is not to pressure them and make them feel like they're not good enough. You're tracking them to see how you can support their development. So don't rush your child into becoming a runner when they're still learning to crawl.

Conclusion

Of all the jobs that exist to date, parenting continues to be one that is riddled with challenges, twists and turns, and emotional highs and lows. There are so many things to be concerned about regarding how your child grows and develops. You only get a chance to be a parent with any particular child once, and the last thing you want to do is mess it up. So, naturally, you will be nervous and have some trepidation regarding this topic. Today, many values, milestones, and benchmarks indicate certain expectations, which can be a little too overwhelming. You may find yourself giving into the temptation to compare where your child is in life versus other children. Remember, your child is far different from any other, so it would be unreasonable to ask them to develop at the same pace as other children and unfair to make comparisons. As their primary caregiver, you must maintain a positive disposition and remain patient as your child develops into a full-fledged human being. This is not a sprint. It is a marathon, and you must act accordingly.

Play therapy is an excellent way for your child to explore, learn, and grow. With it, you will see their innate identity and that they have the potential to develop into a wonderful person. By using play therapy, your child will be able to express themselves and communicate with others as naturally as possible. In the process of playing, they will become more aware of who they are and learn all about their feelings and how they can handle them. They will be at peace with their choices and understand the processes that led them to be who they are. As their caregiver, you play a crucial role in offering your child support as they continue to progress through life.

One of the major benefits of play therapy is teaching your child to become autonomous, both in and out of the sessions. Your child can be the one in charge of their therapy and should be. There's no room for you to force your opinions on them. The only thing you have a say in is the objective that you would like them to accomplish. How the child accomplishes this in a play therapy session is entirely up to them. You must learn to trust that your child has the innate ability to figure out their development journey at their own pace and in their own way. They have their own unique rhythm, and they will accomplish the goals you've set only when it's time.

You'll have to make peace with the challenges you'll face and do your best to handle them head-on. It's all a natural part of growing up. You just need to be as understanding and supportive as possible and recall that your child's progress is not something that you can rush through. They are not in competition with anyone. It is a personal journey for them, and you must be patient as they discover themselves and develop as a result.

Your job as the primary caregiver or parent is to ensure that they are in a nurturing and supportive environment. You want to make sure they have room to communicate freely with you, that you actively pay attention to them, and that you validate every one of their emotions. Creating the sort of safe, non-critical environment your child needs makes it easier for them to express their concerns, fears, hopes, and dreams. So, you should encourage them to explore the world around them and the one within. Have them celebrate when they've accomplished something, and gently guide them when they feel a little bit lost. That way, you'll be well on your way to turning an adorable little human into a lovely person full of warmth and love.

Check out another book in the series

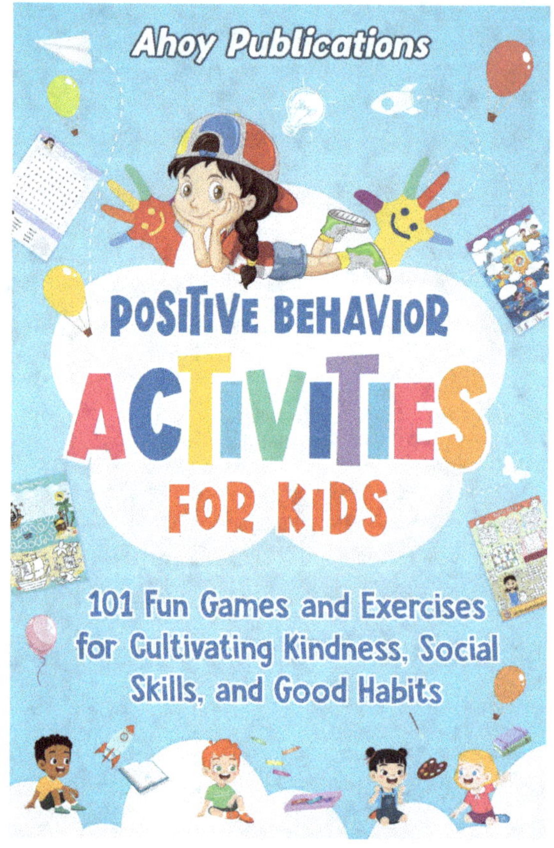

References

(N.d.). Backstage.com. https://www.backstage.com/magazine/article/great-acting-games-for-kids-73608/

(N.d.). Nih.gov. https://www.nimh.nih.gov/health/publications/the-teen-brain-7-things-to-know#:~:text=Although%20the%20brain%20stops%20growing,the%20last%20parts%20to%20mature.

25 easy crafts for toddlers (craft ideas for 2-4 year Olds). (2023, January 9). Craftulate. https://craftulate.com/crafts-for-toddlers/

5 benefits of dance for early childhood development. (2021, June 2). Jooki. https://blog.jooki.com/5-benefits-of-dance-for-early-childhood-development/

6 benefits of preschool performing arts classes for your child. (2022, February 3). Expression City. https://expressioncity.com/6-benefits-of-preschool-performing-arts-classes-for-your-child/

6 fantastic benefits of arts & crafts for kids. (2021, April 4). Tinybeans. https://tinybeans.com/benefits-of-arts-and-crafts-for-kids/

Beck, C. (2022, May 3). Outdoor sensory activities. The OT Toolbox. https://www.theottoolbox.com/outdoor-sensory-diet-activities/

Bergeron, J. (2022, April 1). 20 outdoor sensory play activities for young children + free printable. Active For Life. https://activeforlife.com/20-outdoor-sensory-play-activities/

Breathnach, T. (2020, July 27). 20 amazing things to do outdoors with your preschooler. MadeForMums. https://www.madeformums.com/toddler-and-preschool/20-amazing-things-to-do-outdoors-with-your-pre-schooler/

Browder, A. (2020, February 19). Children are born creative. The Open School | A Self-Directed Democratic School; The Open School. https://www.openschooloc.com/2020/02/19/children-are-born-creative/

Burt, P. (2023, May 4). 30+ arts and crafts ideas for toddlers of 2 and 3 years. Gathered. https://www.gathered.how/arts-crafts/crafts-for-toddlers/

Camille. (2019, April 29). Why Teamwork is Important for Children. Reason Future Tech. https://www.tryreason.com/blog/why-teamwork-is-important-for-children/

Caroline. (2017, September 14). Handprint and footprint baby art project. I Heart Crafty Things. https://iheartcraftythings.com/baby-art-project.html

Cinelli, E. (2022, November 7). 5 quiet activities your child can do instead of napping. Verywell Family. https://www.verywellfamily.com/quiet-time-activities-for-toddlers-6822436

Collage: activity for children 2-6 years. (2022, April 15). Raising Children Network. https://raisingchildren.net.au/guides/activity-guides/making-and-building/collage-activity-for-children-2-6-years

Comments, 0. (2020a, May 13). Egg carton caterpillar craft. My Bored Toddler. https://myboredtoddler.com/egg-carton-caterpillar-craft/

Comments, 0. (2020b, July 17). Butterfly kite toddler craft. My Bored Toddler. https://myboredtoddler.com/butterfly-kite-toddler-craft/

Creating Rhythm ..... A Gift of Love for Your Child. (n.d.). Eblity.com. https://www.eblity.com/special-education-blog/creating-rhythm-a-gift-of-love-for-your-child

Cruz, R. (2022, August 12). 30 cooking activities with toddlers! Teaching Expertise; dontan. https://www.teachingexpertise.com/classroom-ideas/cooking-activities-with-toddlers

Days, S. (2022, March 23). 10 fun cooking activities for toddlers. Sunnydayssunshinecenter.com. https://www.sunnydayssunshinecenter.com/blog/educational-kitchen-activities-toddlers

Della Bitta, A. (2023, April 17). 27 adorable toddler crafts you can pull out anytime. Tinybeans. https://tinybeans.com/arts-and-crafts-for-toddlers/

Dewar, G. (2021, September 11). Evidence-based social skills activities for children and teens (with teaching tips). PARENTING SCIENCE; Gwen Dewar. https://parentingscience.com/social-skills-activities/

Educatall. (2014, May 5). Exploring nature and the outdoors. Educatall. https://www.educatall.com/page/685/Exploring-nature-and-the-outdoors---.html

Erie County Care Management (ECCM). (n.d.). Growing Minds With Cognitive Development Activities for Toddlers. Eccm.Org. https://www.eccm.org/blog/cognitive-development-activities-for-toddlers

Explorers, E. (2019, December 6). 5 Reasons why you should let your child go barefoot. Eco Explorers. https://www.ecoexplorers.com.au/5-reasons-why-you-should-let-your-child-go-barefoot/

Exploring the benefits of sensory play. (n.d.). Goodstart Corporate. https://www.goodstart.org.au/parenting/exploring-the-benefits-of-sensory-play

Five reasons why creativity is important for kids – Studio Jocelyn. (n.d.). Studiojocelyn.Nl. https://www.studiojocelyn.nl/five-reasons-why-creativity-is-important-for-kids/

Garoo, R. (2021, January 27). 23 Best Cognitive Activities For Toddlers Development. MomJunction. https://www.momjunction.com/articles/cognitive-development-activities-for-toddlers_00704930/

Gravenell, A. (n.d.). The many benefits of arts and crafts for children. Kent-teach.com. https://www.kent-teach.com/Blog/post/2021/06/28/the-many-benefits-of-arts-and-crafts-for-children.aspx

Hantak, K., & van der Graaf, V. (n.d.). Why sensory play is important. Communityplaythings.co.uk. https://www.communityplaythings.co.uk/learning-library/articles/the-importance-of-sensory-play

Happiest Baby Staff. (2021, August 12). 6 Low-Fuss Cognitive Activities for Toddlers. Happiest Baby. https://www.happiestbaby.com/blogs/toddler/cognitive-activities-toddlers

How books develop fine motor skills. (n.d.). Babysparks.com. https://babysparks.com/2020/03/09/how-books-develop-fine-motor-skills/

How music and dance can boost your child's confidence and self-esteem. (2023, April 5). SaPa India Blogs; Subramanium Academy of Performing Arts. https://blog.sapaindia.com/how-music-and-dance-can-boost-your-childs-confidence-and-self-esteem/

Hul, J. V. (2022, December 5). How to make blot art hearts. The Artful Parent. https://artfulparent.com/heart-symmetry-painting/

Hul, J. V. (2023a, March 26). How to do watercolor resist crayon art. The Artful Parent. https://artfulparent.com/watercolor-resist-art-with-young-children/

Hul, J. V. (2023b, June 12). 7 simple arts and crafts ideas for toddlers. The Artful Parent. https://artfulparent.com/7-simple-art-activities-for-toddlers

Importance of Art and Craft. (2021, July 20). Classover. https://classover.com/en/blog/importance-of-art-and-craft/

Kids, B. (2019, November 3). The impact of creative play on the brain. The Brain Workshop. https://www.thebrainworkshop.com/blog/the-impact-of-creative-play-on-the-brain/

Kingston, T. (2023, February 12). 75 fun indoor games for kids – boredom busters for all ages. Family Fun Twin Cities. https://www.familyfuntwincities.com/indoor-games-for-kids/

Kitchen science experiments for kids ages 3 to 8. (n.d.). KiwiCo. https://www.kiwico.com/diy/lists/kitchen-science-experiments-for-kids-ages-3-to-8

Kristina. (2021, May 30). Quiet time activities for toddlers and preschoolers. Toddler Approved; Toddler Approved - Simple hands-on activities for busy parents. https://toddlerapproved.com/quiet-time-activities-for-toddlers-and-preschoolers/

Li, P. (2016, December 18). Benefits of sensory play and 21 sensory activities for preschoolers. Parenting For Brain. https://www.parentingforbrain.com/sensory-activities-importance-sensory-play/

Lindner, B. (2019, April 10). Preschool scavenger hunts: Learning through observation. Scholastic.com; Scholastic Parents. https://www.scholastic.com/parents/school-success/learning-toolkit-blog/preschool-scavenger-hunts-learning-through-observation.html

Liz. (2023, June 5). 100+ fun quiet time games and activities for kids. Kids Activities Blog. https://kidsactivitiesblog.com/60561/quiet-time-activities/

London, A. in. (2017, February 23). 15 games & exercises to improve acting skills (taught in drama schools). Acting in London. https://actinginlondon.co.uk/exercises-improve-acting-skills/

Makvana, H. (2015, August 24). 21 fun indoor games for kids aged 3 to 12 years. MomJunction. https://www.momjunction.com/articles/indoor-games-and-kids-activities-for-this-season_00369105/

Marshall-Seslar, A. (2022, January 20). 8 Engaging Cognitive Development Activities for Toddlers. Wellbeingswithalysia.Com. https://wellbeingswithalysia.com/cognitive-development-activities-toddlers/

McClelland, S. (2022, January 31). Salt painting for kids. Little Bins for Little Hands. https://littlebinsforlittlehands.com/salt-painting/

McClelland, S. (2023, July 9). 35 best kitchen science experiments. Little Bins for Little Hands. https://littlebinsforlittlehands.com/4-mini-easiest-kitchen-science-activity-trays/

Mcilroy, T. (2019, May 10). 9 fun music games for kids that are excellent for development. Empowered Parents. https://empoweredparents.co/music-games-for-kids/

Meg. (2023, January 17). 16 (screen-free!) quiet time activities for toddlers. The Toddler Playbook. https://thetoddlerplaybook.com/16-quiet-activity-ideas-for-toddlers-preschoolers/

Michelle. (2023, February 5). Paper crown craft for kids. Taming Little Monsters. https://taminglittlemonsters.com/paper-crown-craft-for-kids/

Miley. (2018, December 14). 10 best improv games for kids. ChildFun. https://www.childfun.com/recommendations/best-improv-games-for-kids/

Millacci, T. S. (2022, January 18). 16 activities to stimulate emotional development in children. Positivepsychology.com. https://positivepsychology.com/emotional-development-activities/

MSU extension. (2017, May 15). MSU Extension. https://www.canr.msu.edu/news/children_and_empathy_teamwork

Occupational Therapy Helping Children. (2023, May 12). Social interaction in play milestones: What you need to know. Occupational Therapy Helping Children. https://occupationaltherapy.com.au/social-interaction-in-play-milestones-what-you-need-to-know/

Ostrosky, M. M., Yang, H.-W., & Stalega, M. (n.d.). Let's get moving: Using children's literature to support physical activity and readiness skills. Eric.ed.gov. https://files.eric.ed.gov/fulltext/ED582061.pdf

Pelly, J. (2020, June 15). Sensory play: 20 great activities for your toddler or preschooler. Healthline. https://www.healthline.com/health/childrens-health/sensory-play

Pieterse, L. (2022, March 30). 25 fantastic improv games for students. Teaching Expertise; dontan. https://www.teachingexpertise.com/classroom-ideas/improv-games/

Playdough activities: children 3-6 years. (2023, May 9). Raising Children Network. https://raisingchildren.net.au/guides/activity-guides/making-and-building/playdough-activities

Pummill, L. (2020, October 21). Patty Case Paper Plate Fish. My Bored Toddler. https://myboredtoddler.com/patty-case-paper-plate-fish/

Pummill, L. (2022, June 29). Paper cup whale. My Bored Toddler. https://myboredtoddler.com/paper-cup-whale/

Pummill, L. (2023, June 16). Fork flower painting. My Bored Toddler. https://myboredtoddler.com/fork-flower-painting/

Reimer, J. (2022, October 30). Preschoolers quiet time activities perfect for 4 year old's - HOAWG. Hands On As We Grow®. https://handsonaswegrow.com/quiet-activities-for-preschoolers/

Sarah. (2022, June 15). 43 Quiet Time activities for 2 year Olds - how wee learn. How Wee Learn - Out of the Box Learning Ideas, Playful Art, Exploring Nature, and Simple Living - That Is How We Learn! https://www.howweelearn.com/quiet-time-activites-2-year-olds/

Shakibaie, S. (2019, March 27). Sensory play: Benefits, ideas & activities. Ready Kids. https://readykids.com.au/sensory-play-for-childhood-development-and-learning/

Sitters.co.uk - the 15 best activities for children to learn through play. (n.d.). Www.sitters.co.uk. https://www.sitters.co.uk/blog/the-15-best-activities-for-children-to-help-them-learn-through-play.aspx

Stockdale, G. (2022, January 15). 6 reasons why art and crafts are so important for child development - ActivityBox. ActivityBox - Learn Creative Thinking the Fun Way; ActivityBox. https://activity-box.com/6-reasons-why-art-and-crafts-are-so-important-for-child-development

Subramani, A. (2020, September 7). Exploring the benefits of sensory play for children. Only About Children. https://www.oac.edu.au/news-views/sensory-play/

Sue. (2021, March 27). 40+ music and movement activities for toddlers and preschoolers. The Montessori-Minded Mom; Reachformontessori.com. https://reachformontessori.com/music-and-movement-activities/

The importance of teamwork for your child - oasis summer day camps. (2022, April 14). Oasischildren.com; Oasis Summer Day Camps. https://oasischildren.com/the-importance-of-teamwork-for-your-child/

Thinking and play: toddlers. (2022, December 20). Raising Children Network. https://raisingchildren.net.au/toddlers/play-learning/play-toddler-development/thinking-play-toddlers

Thompson, T. (2018, January 24). 10 ways to explore nature in winter. Creative Family Fun. https://creativefamilyfun.net/10-ways-to-explore-nature-in-winter/

Tips for keeping infants and toddlers safe: A developmental guide for home visitors – toddlers. (n.d.). ECLKC. https://eclkc.ohs.acf.hhs.gov/safety-practices/article/tips-keeping-infants-toddlers-safe-developmental-guide-home-visitors-toddlers

Today's Parent. (2019, November 12). Best indoor games for kids - today's parent. Today's Parent; SJC Media. https://www.todaysparent.com/toddler/20-fun-indoor-games/

Vanstone, E. (2021, March 11). Kitchen science experiments for kids - 50 awesome experiments. Science Experiments for Kids; Science Sparks. https://www.science-sparks.com/kitchen-science-round-up/

What is sensory play and why is it important? (n.d.). Action for Children. https://www.actionforchildren.org.uk/blog/what-is-sensory-play-and-why-is-it-important/

Why learning through drama is beneficial to child development. (n.d.). The Learning Connections. https://tlc.com.sg/why-learning-through-drama-is-beneficial-to-child-development/

Withers, R. (2019, August 23). Easy yarn suncatchers for kids. The Artful Parent. https://artfulparent.com/easy-yarn-suncatchers-for-kids/

Withers, R. (2022, June 25). Painting with bubble wrap for kids. The Artful Parent. https://artfulparent.com/painting-with-bubble-wrap-for-kids/

Withers, R. (2023, June 14). How to paint with cars: Easy action art for kids. The Artful Parent. https://artfulparent.com/painting-with-wheels-is-fun-action-art-for-kids/

American Academy of Family Physicians. (n.d.). How to teach good behavior: Tips for parents. https://www.aafp.org/pubs/afp/issues/2002/1015/p1463.html

As for additional sources on play therapy for toddlers, here are ten books that might be helpful:

Axline, V.M., & Armstrong, H.C. (1969). Play therapy: The inner dynamics of childhood.

Bratton, S.C., Ray, D., Rhine, T., & Jones, L. (2005). The efficacy of play therapy with children: A meta-analytic review of treatment outcomes.

Carmichael, K.D. (2006). Play therapy: An introduction.

Clara. (2022, February 27). 23 Fun Empathy Activities for Kids + (Printable) Kindness Challenge. Very Special Tales. https://veryspecialtales.com/empathy-activities-for-kids-printable-kindness/

Edutopia. (n.d.). Integrating music into social and emotional learning. https://www.edutopia.org/article/integrating-music-social-and-emotional-learning

Foran, L. M. (2009). Listening to music: Helping children regulate their emotions and improve learning in the classroom. Educational Horizons, 88(1), 51-58. https://files.eric.ed.gov/fulltext/EJ868339.pdf

Gil, E., & Drewes, A.A. (2005). Cultural issues in play therapy.

Guerney Jr., L.F., & Guerney, B.G. (1997). Child-centered play therapy.

Healthline (n.d.). Sensory Play: 20 Great Activities for Your Toddler or Preschooler. https://www.healthline.com/health/childrens-health/sensory-play

Homeyer, L.E., & Morrison, M.O. (2008). Play therapy practices, issues, and trends: A sourcebook.

https://www.facebook.com/parents. (2022). The Secret Language of Toddlers: What Their Behaviors Mean. Parents. https://www.parents.com/toddlers-preschoolers/development/behavioral/what-toddler-behavior-means/

https://www.verywellmind.com/play-therapy-definition-types-techniques-5194915

https://www.verywellmind.com/child-development-theories-2795068

Kaduson, H.G., & Schaefer, C.E. (2006). 101 favorite play therapy techniques.

Landreth, G.L., & Bratton, S.C. (1999). Child-centered play therapy.

O'Connor, K.J., & Schaefer, C.E. (1994). Handbook of play therapy.

PositivePsychology.com. (n.d.). 16 activities to stimulate emotional development in children. https://positivepsychology.com/emotional-development-activities/

Rasmussen University (n.d.). 25 Sensational Sensory Activities for Toddlers - Rasmussen University. https://www.rasmussen.edu/degrees/education/blog/sensory-activities-for-toddlers/

Schaefer, C.E., & O'Connor, K.J. (1983). Handbook of Play Therapy

www.ingramcontent.com/pod-product-compliance
Lightning Source LLC
Chambersburg PA
CBHW082019150726
48196CB00073B/548